Cases in Organisational Behaviour

Lecturer's Guide

Edited by Derek Adam-Smith
and Alan Peacock

PITMAN
PUBLISHING

KV-241-645

PITMAN PUBLISHING
128 Long Acre, London WC2E 9AN

A Division of Longman Group UK Limited

First published in 1994

© Derek Adam-Smith and Alan Peacock 1994

Copyright © Case 1 Laurie Mullins and Ian White 1994
Copyright © Case 2 Dolores Thomson Yong 1994
Copyright © Case 3 Joanna Brewis 1994
Copyright © Case 4 Linda Hicks 1994
Copyright © Case 5 Per Darmer 1994
Copyright © Case 6 Henner Hentze 1994
Copyright © Case 7 Robert Jones and Peter Gal 1994
Copyright © Case 8 Sarah L. Henson and Fred Turner 1994
Copyright © Case 9 Pernille Eskerod and Per Darmer 1994
Copyright © Case 10 K.Alan Rutter 1994
Copyright © Case 11 Karen Meudell 1994
Copyright © Case 12 Jeff Watling 1994
Copyright © Case 13 Linda Keen 1994
Copyright © Case 14 Derek Adam-Smith and Alex Littlewood 1994
Copyright © Case 15 Roger Page and Alan Peacock 1994
Copyright © Case 16 David Yong and Tony Emerson 1994
Copyright © Case 17 Gary Akehurst 1994
Copyright © Case 18 David Goss 1994
Copyright © Case 19 David Farnham 1994
Copyright © Case 20 Alan Peacock 1994
Copyright © Case 21 Irene Watson 1994
Copyright © Case 22 Marjorie Corbridge and Stephen Pilbeam 1994
Copyright © Case 23 Tom McEwan 1994
Copyright © Case 24 Jeff Watling and Tony Strike 1994
Copyright © Case 25 Karen Meudell and Tony Callen 1994
Copyright © Case 26 Brian McCormack and Linda McCormack 1994
Copyright © Case 27 David Goss 1994

A CIP catalogue record for this book can be obtained from the British Library.

ISBN 0 273 60449 X

All rights reserved; no part of this publication may be reproduced,stored
in a retrieval system, or transmitted in any form or by any means, electronic,
mechanical, photocopying, recording, or otherwise without either the prior
written permission of the Publishers or a licence permitting restricted copying
in the United Kingdom issued by the Copyright Licensing Agency Ltd,
90 Tottenham Court Road, London W1P 9HE. This book may not be lent,
resold, hired out or otherwise disposed of by way of trade in any form
of binding or cover other than that in which it is published,
without the prior consent of the Publishers.

Printed and bound in Great Britain

The Publishers' policy is to use paper manufactured from sustainable forests.

Introduction

The collection of cases contained in the book, *Cases in Organisational Behaviour*, is designed to support the use of texts covering theories that attempt to explain people's behaviour in organisations. The cases are offered to tutors as a means of exploring with students how such theories may be applied in the quest for solutions to real-life problems. As the Introduction to the book suggests, managers are currently working in a highly complex environment and few incidents are likely to relate to a single issue. However, the cases have been grouped in a way which reflects their main themes and the activity briefs pose questions which the contributors believe explore the key issues facing those seeking to deal with the problems highlighted by the case. Other themes covered by a case, beyond its main topic, are shown in the matrix.

This Lecturer's Guide contains information provided by the contributors to assist tutors in the use of the cases. The uniqueness of each case is reflected in the structure of the authors' comments. However, the notes on each case seek to relate the issues it explores to relevant organisational behaviour theory, provide suggestions on how the material may be used and, where appropriate, indicate what happened to the problem in practice. In particular, each contributor has provided notes on answers to the questions set in the activity brief. These are indicative rather than definitive answers. While we expect, and hope, that tutors and students will wish to develop their own ideas from the material, the guide does provide structured and informed support to the cases.

The recommended reading for each case has been chosen from books and journals which should be readily accessible to students. In some cases the contributors believe that other references may be of interest to tutors and these have been included under the heading of Further reading in the guide to each case.

The successful achievement of an organisation's goals is heavily dependent upon its managers' ability to understand the interrelated factors that influence people's behaviour at work. We believe the cases presented in the book, together with the information contained in this guide, provide an opportunity to apply this understanding to the challenging issues currently facing practising and potential managers.

Derek Adam-Smith
Alan Peacock

Part 1
Management and Organisational Behaviour

Case 1

APPLICATIONS OF ORGANISATION THEORY IN HELGATON LIMITED

Laurie Mullins and Ian White

Introduction

Writing on organisation and management in some form or another can be traced back thousands of years. This has led to many developments in management theory focusing on a whole range of organisational issues. However, when managers make decisions that affect the organisation they are unlikely to consult reference texts containing complex theories before they act. Rather their judgements are more likely to be based on a combination of past experiences and acquired knowledge. This knowledge is made up of many sources of information — including academic theories. Organisation theory can be seen therefore as part of the total pool of knowledge from which managers base their future judgements and actions.

How this case can be used

This case study provides the opportunity to evaluate an attempt to assess the practical use and applicability of organisation theory within a modern commercial organisation.
The questions can be used as the basis for both written assignments and small group discussion. In addition, participants can be asked to contrast the results and conclusions of their analysis with applications of organisation theory within their own organisation.

Learning Objectives

The learning objectives of this case include:
- To promote an understanding of the complex nature of organisational behaviour and management theory.
- To assess the value of the study of management theory and different approaches to organisation and management.
- To evaluate the relationship between the development of theory and management practice.
- To recognise the difficulties and limitations with this form of investigation.

Question 1

Comment critically on the nature and value of the investigation. What difficulties does such an investigation present and how might these difficulties be best overcome?

Matters for discussion could include the following.
- Size and range of the population sample, and balance of males/females.

- Many alternative approaches for the analysis of organisation theory, for example the adoption of a sociological perspective which argues that people have their own goals at work.
- Difficulties of objective measurement and the extent to which discovery of meaning is based on interpretation and intuition.
- The reliability and validity of: (i) the interviews as an interactive situation; and (ii) the secondary data which originates from within the organisation.
- The effects of cultural influences in a modern business organisation.
- Reasons for limited responses to certain questions such as: 11. The Larger Environment; 13. Personal Goals at Work; and 19. Prediction of Behaviour.
- In what ways might the wording of the questions and conduct of the interview be improved? To what extent might certain questions be best addressed using direct observation?

Question 2

State clearly the conclusions you draw from the investigation and discuss the extent to which it reveals practical applications of organisation theory.

The multiplicity of studies of organisations has led to a wide and diverse range of theories. In order to help identify main trends in the development of organisational behaviour and management theory it is helpful therefore to have some framework in which to analyse contrasting approaches to improving organisational performance and effectiveness. One such framework which could serve as the basis for discussion of applications of organisation theory is that suggested by Mullins which identifies the four main approaches of:
- Classical;
- Human Relations;
- Systems;
- Contingency.

Classical could include considerations of the clear definition of duties, `the one best way' principle, extent of specialisation, the planning of work and bureaucratic structure.
Human Relations could include considerations of the importance of the five factors in Q.18 (output, groups and leadership, communications, motivation, job design), management style, training and employee satisfaction.
Systems could include considerations of environmental influences, effects of technology, and the balance between technical requirements and management skills.
Contingency could include considerations of the concept of the Autonomous Work Group and importance of teamwork, organisation structure, and managerial responsive to change.

It is important to remember however that the various approaches represent a progression of ideas and together provide a pattern of complementary studies into the development of organisation theory. Any categorisation is somewhat arbitrary and it is possible to identify a number of other approaches. For example an additional basis of analysis could be the Social

Action approach and consideration of such matters as, for example, personal goals at work and commitment to a common purpose.

Although the practical applications are not always recognised overtly, managers apply organisation theory everyday. The investigation at Helgaton Ltd. can also be seen as a basis for debating the suppositions that: (i) organisation theory is actively applied but only at a subconscious level; and (ii) that at least some elements of all the different approaches are likely to found in most organisations.

Helgaton Ltd could be seen to have a mixed organisation structure: for example classical principles apply to policies and procedures and the task, generating a 'mechanistic' system; while an 'organic' system is applied to the people issue.

Question 3

Explain and justify the specific recommendations you would make to the top management of Helgaton Ltd as a result of the investigation.

- It is important to avoid the danger of classical/scientific management principles becoming a controlling device and endangering the 'empowering' process.
- Clarify implementation of Role, Responsibilities and Objectives and the managers' perception relating to achieving goals at work.
- Particular attention should be given to the responses to Q.18 on importance of various factors. For example the importance attached to groups and leadership, and greater attention to job design linked to employee satisfaction and the perceived reduced opportunities for promotion.
- Motivation and rewards systems should be related to the philosophy about empowerment, working in teams and the concept of the autonomous work group.
- Review the structure of the organisation and the extent to which it is perceived to be hierarchical.
- Although secondary data can provide useful information it should be treated just as the names implies. For example the limited reference in the interviews to the employee survey. Greater attention should be given to the actual beliefs, perceptions and actions of people.

Further reading

Handy, C. B. (1993). *Understanding Organizations*, Fourth Edition, Harmondsworth: Penguin.

Huczynski, A. A. and Buchanan D. A. (1991). *Organizational Behaviour: An Introductory Text*, Second Edition, Hemel Hempstead: Prentice-Hall.

Mullins, L. J. (1993). *Management and Organisational Behaviour*, Third Edition, London: Pitman.

Pugh, D. S. (Ed) (1990). *Organization Theory: Selected Readings*, Third Edition, Harmondsworth: Penguin.

Robbins, S. P. (1993). *Organizational Behavior*, Sixth Edition, New Jersey: Prentice-Hall.

Wilson, D. C. and Rosenfeld, R. H. (1990). *Managing Organizations: text, readings and cases*, Maidenhead: McGraw-Hill.

Case 2

SENTOSA ENGINEERING — MANAGING IN AN EASTERN CULTURE

Dolores Thomson Yong

This case describes an extremely complex situation in which all participants suffer from stress. The causes of this can be assessed through an examination of different facets of the situation. There are organisational problems both formal and informal. In a fast developing economy which is experiencing rapid industrialisation for the first time, an organisation is bound to incur the pains of formalisation and growth. Added to this is the meeting of Western management and Eastern colleagues and workers. The lack of attention to detail in human relations leads directly to threats to the organisation's survival.

The external environment is also experiencing rapid change. To some extent the organisation's problems are tied in with the economic changes facing a society in which achievement is much emphasised and whose fulfillment leads to additional complications. The Republic has been experiencing high labour turnover on account of demand exceeding supply. This situation is made worse by the Eastern characteristic of not attempting to resolve interpersonal problems which leads to open conflict between employees. The implication is that employees are left with no options other than leaving or greater stress if they remain with the organisation. Western management theories (Maslow, Herzberg etc.) all advocate employee participation. To what extent can inherent cultural tendencies be eradicated? Eastern employees are reluctant to question a superior's decision-making since this can often imply insubordination. It is interesting to note that the Japanese practice of group decision-making (as in quality circles) has become more acceptable in Singapore. In this way the individual can camouflage his/her individuality with the group and individuals are not seen to be challenging or questioning senior management.

The case also presents material for cross-cultural management assumptions. Management training is much sought after in the Republic. Nearly all books are American or UK based. Few efforts are made to demonstrate the need for the society to discriminate in their absorption of management literature. Yet fundamentally, the local culture and work attitudes are dissimilar to that in the countries mentioned.

What steps can Western management personnel undertake in order to adapt to local conditions? Which assumptions apply/do not apply?

Finally, all Eastern and Western personnel involved find themselves in managerial activity with little or no formal training. Their expertise seems to lie in technical areas. It is no surprise that managerial, and in particular human relations problems seem overbearing. Would the professionally trained manager fare better? What are the pitfalls a fully experienced and trained manager could avoid?

How the case can be used

This case can be used to examine problems in formalising structure in a climate of inexperience and rapid expansion. An additional point of focus is the multi-cultural interplay between Western and Eastern attitudes. Such an interplay has accentuated human relations problems which are already inevitable given the complex circumstances. Suggested learning objectives are:

- To emphasise the importance of defined organisation structure and functions.
- To ensure that all concerned are aware of objectives and strategies.
- To demonstrate that sensitive communications can off-set much confusion and stress.
- To show the importance of training in the management of people — especially in the personnel management function.
- To examine and evaluate the necessity for cross-cultural briefing before undertaking management positions in a different culture.
- To become aware of general problems in organisations undergoing rapid growth and change.

Guidance for Answers

The following points are provided as a basis for answering the first three questions:

(a)   Participants are directed to use their knowledge of popular theories from behavioural schools (Maslow, Herzberg etc) to demonstrate problems arising from Theory X management practice. This applies to both Eastern and Western managers. Participants can bring into the discussion all their learning on the points concerning good management in the area of planning and control. (For example, Child's three main design choices concerning centralisation/decentralisation, degree of formality/informality, and span of control.) These concepts can be applied to such management issues as authority, responsibility and delegation.

(b)   Traditional views on management leadership can be examined to assess the appropriateness of the practice described in the case. An excursion through the wide field on 'leadership' thinking should generate choice of styles which suit. (McGregor's Theory X, Blake and Mouten, Ouchi etc.). A useful framework for examination could be Rensis likert's four styles:

        exploitative authoritative
        benevolent authoritative
        consultative authoritative
        participative group management

and their application to the situation at Sentosa Engineering

(c)   The cause of much stress, culminating in high labour turnover, seems to arise from lack of proper channels of communication. Basic assumptions on good communications techniques can be covered here. Participants can select problems arising from poor communications provision. Solutions lie in how far effective communication can develop 'trust' between senior management and subordinates.

(d)   Participants should be directed to focus on local attitudes and culture. Problems are complex in such a sensitive cross-cultural background. Expatriate management must be sensitive to local rivalries and status symbols. Are the American and European philosophy of management universally applicable? That aspect of management which lacks universality has to do with interpersonal relationships, including those between management and workers, management and the community/ Government. Participants may like to examine the Kootz model which shows that universal management fundamentals are still tenable. Factors which should be taken into account are educational, sociological and political constraints.

The role playing exercise is designed to encourage participants to empathize with the situation and problems. In so doing solutions to labour turnover problems would utilise all principles referred to in question the section above.

Case 3

THE ROLE OF INTIMACY AT WORK: INTERACTIONS AND RELATIONSHIPS IN THE MODERN ORGANISATION

Joanna Brewis

How the case can be used

This case study provides empirical background for an introduction to bureaucracy theory, and what could be said to be its polar opposite ('Excellence' theory). Learning objectives include:

- The awareness that relationships between individuals in the workplace form a part of and reinforce organizational culture, and that regulation in organizations is not necessarily formalised.

- A knowledge of the strengths and weaknesses of bureaucracy theory.

- The understanding that cultures differ hugely, even (as is the case in the study), within one organization.

- An awareness that the industrial environment which supported bureaucratic organizations is arguably declining, and being replaced by a different (post)industrial form.

- Some knowledge of the methods of the 'Excellence' gurus.

- The understanding that 'real life' organizations cannot always be easily 'pigeonholed'.

Theory relevant to the case study

Department A in the case study could be said to approximate closely to the Weberian (1948) model of bureaucracy. As an organization, it is structured hierarchically, relationships within it being characterized by a high degree of impersonality, and the cohering force within the department being that of the teaching and research it conducts. Harrison (1987) describes such a workplace as possessing a 'role' culture, the components of which mirror those of the ideal-type bureaucracy. Department B on the other hand is arguably more of a 'support' culture; relationships are far more personalized, rather than individuals reacting to each other on the basis of departmental role. Contemporary theory (e.g. Harrison (ibid); Peters 1989; Kanter 1989) advocates that today's economic conditions lend themselves better to the latter — that rapidly changing technology, globalization, fragmentation of markets and the transition to a service-based economy mean that bureaucratic organizations are (i) too rigid to respond to change and (ii) do not engender the necessary workforce commitment to allow for peak organizational performance.

The case study also raises the issue of the impact of organizational culture on individuals (rather than simply the achievement of organizational goals), and by so doing provides an alternative way to 'read' organizational behaviour. This relates to the paradigmatic approach outlined by Morgan (1986).

Guidance for answers

Question 1(a)

According to bureaucracy theory, what kind of personal relationships should exist between organizational participants? Draw upon the case for illustration.

Students should provide a formulation of ideal-type bureaucracy in response to this question, that which is based around the principle that human 'irrationality' interferes with the efficient operation of organizations. Hence bureaucracy as originally formulated by Weber seeks to routinise all interactions, appoint on the basis of qualifications rather than personality and erect strict lines of command. Support for these theoretical principles can be drawn from the case study; for example the professor who sends memos rather than picking up the phone for an informal chat.

Question 1(b)

How might the above model impact on

(i) individuals and
(ii) the achievement of organizational goals?

Draw upon the case for illustration.

This question provides the opportunity for students to reflect on the difference between theoretical recommendations and empirical 'reality'. Weber claimed that bureaucracy was the most technically excellent form of organization possible, because it precludes the possibility of human error and provides guidelines for every eventuality. However, empirical evidence shows that this is not necessarily the case; various authors have demonstrated the negative effects of bureaucracy, for example, Merton's bureaucratic personality, the encouragement of minimum acceptable behaviour as identified by Gouldner. Furthermore, Weber himself was dubious about the possibly dehumanizing and alienating effects of the bureaucracy on the individuals working within it; dubbing it the 'iron cage'. The case study illustrates both organizational and human effects of bureaucracy; the inability of one professor to deal with disciplinary matters for example, or the complaint that there is no understanding whatsoever in Department A. It is also the case that bureaucracy has its supporters however: the women whose experience leads them to feel that a more 'cosy' atmosphere encourages sexual harassment for example.

Question 2(a)

Contemporary management theories advocate a different mode of interaction within the workplace. How does it differ from that described above? What is the rationale behind such recommendations?

Harrison (1987: pp 2-3) puts this particularly evocatively; he asks us to:

> 'share a vision of work as a healing and growthful experience and organizations as healthy places for humans to become the best they can be.'

This philosophy mirrors that of the Human Relations theorists of the early twentieth century; recognition at work engenders commitment to organizational goals. It also has its roots in Japanese management techniques. The same ideas are to be found in Peters and Waterman (1982) and Peters (1989) — that hierarchies should be flattened, team-working encouraged and every individual made to feel that they are a valuable part of the workforce through being listened to. These strategies then secure increased standards of service/production and co-operation in the face of the economic pressures identified in the Theory Relevant to the Case Study section, as opposed to the resentment and detachment often fostered by bureaucracy. It seems important at this point to also discuss whether students feel that it is morally appropriate for managers to attempt to secure employee loyalty for the sake of increased profit, as it were.

Question 2(b)

Would you say that Department B demonstrates the characteristics of the new workplace as envisaged by the theories above? Support your answer.

To a certain extent Department B could be seen to be a support culture; it is small, friendly and those within it co-operate with each other and react to each other as individuals. However, this culture is not one that is fostered by any deliberate policy, or one that would necessarily endure as the department aged and grew in size. It is also the case that the intimacy in this department breeds gossip, and occasionally unwanted sexual attentions. Furthermore, there is a hierarchy, even if it is not adhered to on a day-to-day basis. Although the individuals in the department are close, this does not mean that their relationships impact on the way they conduct their work; it is more a case of close friendships co-existing with a reasonably structured routine. Individuals of different status can be close friends, but it is unlikely that a superior would consult his subordinate in a work situation.

Question 3

Suggest why the two departments differ in culture. If you were given the task of managing cultural change as suggested by the theories in question 2(a), how might you go about it? Why might current pressures on academia necessitate such a change?

There are several indicators in the text as to why A and B might be so different: size, history and geographical location. Students may also identify other influences on culture, the leadership for example, or the tasks undertaken within the workplace. As for cultural change, students should first of all recognise that this is by no means easy, or quick. Cultural change/ OD steps should perhaps include commitment from senior management to the change, establishing ownership by the workforce (consultation), stripping hierarchical levels, increased communication, creation of semi-autonomous `profit' centres etc. Pressures on academia which might necessitate the change to a more service-orientated culture include funding cuts, U.F.C. gradings and teaching quality assessment exercises, all of which could be seen to result in intensified competition between the institutions.

Further reading

Blau, P. (1963). *The Dynamics of Bureaucracy: A Study of Interpersonal Relationships in Two Government Agencies*, Chicago: University Press, Part 3.

Gouldner, A. (1954). *Patterns of Industrial Bureaucracy*, New York: Free Press, Chapter IX.

Kanter, R.M. (1989). *When Giants Learn to Dance: Mastering the Challenges of Strategy, Management and Careers in the 1990's*, New York: Simon Schuster, conclusion.

Merton, R. (1968). *Social Theory and Social Structure*, New York: Free Press, Chapter VI.

Morgan, G. (1986). *Images of Organization*, London: Sage, Chapter 2.

Ouchi, W.G. (1980). *Theory Z: How American Business Can Meet the Japanese Challenge* Reading. Massachusetts: Addison-Wesley.

Peters, T. and Waterman, S. (1982). *In Search of Excellence: Lessons From America's Best-Run Companies*, New York: Harper & Row, Chapter 8.

Sabel, C.F. & Piore, M.J. (1984). *The Second Industrial Divide: Possibilities for Prosperity*, New York: Basic Books.

Part 2
The Individual, Groups and Leadership

Case 4

THE MYSTERY OF THE DISAPPEARING FEMALE HOTEL GRADUATE

Linda Hicks

How the case can be used

This case lends itself to a variety of teaching and learning styles. It can be considered in its entirety or each section can be studied in greater depth.

At one level the case can be used simply as a vehicle for discussing women's position within hotels. Alternatively it is possible to focus on any one of the three explanations and use the case as a stimulus for additional reading and work assignments. Although the major focus is gender the case links into a range of managerial and cultural issues which would satisfy a number of learning objectives:

- Develop understanding of attitudes; how they are formed, changed and their affect and power within the work place.

- Promote an understanding of the barriers that women face developing a management career.

- Develop understanding of the links between tradition, culture and notions of management and management development.

- Evaluate the policies, processes and practices of management development.

- Identify the importance of the informal network, the subtleties of organisational life and the nature of personal relationships at work, highlighting power and politics within the organisation.

- Promote a discussion of equality within the work place.

The case may be used as straightforward illustration of the problems that women face in their management career; or it can be used as a reference point for other industries with which the processes can be compared or as an illustration of significant management and cultural issues.

Assignments could consist of essays and reports: group work or paired work could have additional benefits particularly if there is a gender-mix. Discussions are considered to be essential for this particular area; they require sensitive handling to ensure that discussions are not just the airing of prejudiced attitudes but are opportunities in which attitudes can be shared, evidence produced and evaluated and recommendations made.

Further information on the case and guidance to answers

The above section provides a context for the questions at the end of the case. The content of the study is based on research for a PhD and at this point it is applicable to indicate some of the major findings:

1.   It is not tenable to suggest that women do not have the same aspirations as men to reach managerial positions.

2.   Elements of hotel work do seem to work against the development of women.

      (a)   Major beliefs about the ways of working exclude women.

      (b)   Men dominate high status operational positions.

      (c)   Who succeeds is largely based on subjective perceptions of personality and character.

      (d)   Hotels have a history of tradition which is resilient to change.

3.   The role of the hotel manager cannot be over-estimated in terms of developing young trainees and in transmitting organisational culture.

A major finding of the research was the degree of consensus which emerged. Managers saw their working world as having demands which were different to all other industries. The fact that hotels do not close led to a series of elaborations and clarification of why things are as they are. Practices became 'obvious' and actions taken for granted — they developed a concrete quality. For instance, presence within the hotel was regarded as essential, to be seen around and to be in a position to perform practical tasks of hotel work was a key management role. Tight management control was seen as a consequence of this action and indeed the lack of trust between management and staff was another universal feature about the hotel world. Power was exercised by managers with regard to the trainees career path both in terms of appraising and developing the trainee. Who you know in the industry was regarded as an essential part of career success. Male and female trainees were expected to follow different career routes; they had different assumptions made of them and the consequences of which ensured that they experienced different levels of monitoring and control. Women were not 'trusted' to perform in the same way as men, neither were they trusted to stay within the hotel industry. Women had to convince management they were serious and genuine about their career in hotel management.

Another point which should be borne in mind is that the sexism displayed by the managers was not always deliberate or intentional but implied as part of their interpretation of hotel management. These interpretations were themselves built on tradition and custom laced with ambiguity.

Question 1

A good answer would note the circularity of the three explanations. A key argument would be the informal network of organisations; emphasis should be given to its power, the interpretation of practices and the self-perpetuation of customs.

The question also asks for alternative and additional reinforcement of gender positions within organisations. Further evidence with regard to the roles of women outside the workplace and the attitudes of managers should therefore be included.

Question 2

Answers should compare male and female career routes with specific illustrations of the ways in which females may be disadvantaged. It would be interesting to compare this female dominated world with a male dominated industry or with another female sector (such as retailing) for similarities and differences in terms of possible barriers and opportunities. Other reasons for success or failure should also be identified (i.e. some women do succeed in this industry and some men do not). Factors such as social class, race, age, education could also be included.

It should of course be noted that women are not disadvantaged in the recruitment and selection procedure. Women do have a place within hotels and 'getting in' is not a problem. (In marked contrast to some industries.)

Question 3

Further reading is recommended for this question. The question does assume some experience of working and if the group is mixed it might be more beneficial to use it as a basis for discussion in the first instance. Focus should be drawn to the interpretive nature of identification and development, the power of certain key individuals and of the informal over the formal processes.

In addition the following could also be discussed: the possible complication of mixed-gender mentoring; emotional dilemmas in the workplace; sexual attractiveness; sexual harassment.

Question 4

The first part of this guide suggests a context in which this question could be answered. It raises the difficulties of studying culture and the ways in which organisational life assumes a 'common-sense' which is totally taken for granted.

Question 5

Reference should be made to the interpretation of tradition and culture in hotels. Folk heroes were also male and it is likely that students will be more aware of the male leaders in the hotel and catering world. Interpretation of the conditions of work and the managerial role has led to an expectation that it fits the male or the exceptional female. Consideration should also be given to the findings of the research given in the section above and a discussion of these points should be raised before the essay is attempted.

Question 6

One of the difficulties of setting such a question is that answers might intimate that if only women could be more like men then their problems would be over! In a good answer the student should reflect on the point that it is the process and its interpretation that requires change. Individualist exhortations do not fundamentally change the culture or the manner of its transmission. Managers of hotels are themselves 'victims' of the cultural context and they are not to blame neither are the women.

Having said that there are certain key recommendations that could be included:

Women should:

(a) Insist on an agreed training and development programme which is continuously monitored and where constructive feedback is given this should aid visibility.

(b) Be self-reflective in their training and disciplined in terms of their own personal development, training needs and required experience.

(c) Communicate their career intentions to the managers in power or if the manager does not hear then build up a relationship with the personnel department at Head Office.

(d) Tackle stereotyped assumptions.

Further reading

Role of Women and Women Managers

Astin H.S. (1984). 'The Meaning of Work in Women's Lives: A Sociopsychological Model of Career Choice and Work Behaviour', *The Counselling Psychologist*, 12 4: 117—126

Davidson M.J. and Cooper C.I. (1992), *Shattering the Glass Ceiling*, Paul Chapman.

Guerrier Y. (1986). 'Hotel Manager: An Unsuitable Job for a Woman', *Service Industries*

Journal, Vol 6, No 2: 227—240

Cultural Context

Deal T.E. and Kennedy A.A. (1982). *Corporate Cultures*, Reading, MA: Addison-Wesley.

Schein E. (1985). *Organisational Culture and Leadership: A Dynamic View*, San Fransisco: Jossey Bass.

Smircich L. (1983). 'Studying Organizations as Cultures' in Morgan G, *Beyond Method: Strategies for Social Research*, Sage.

Managers and Management Development

Gunz H. (1989). *Careers and Corporate Cultures: Managerial Mobility in Large Corporations*, Basil Blackwell: London.

Kotter J.P. (1982). *The General Manager*, New York Free Press.

Stewart R. (1986). *The Reality of Management*, Pan.

Case 5

SAS - MERGERS IN THE AIR?

Per Darmer

The case can be used to highlight a number of aspects of organisational behaviour and international management.

The questions posed can be used to promote discussion, as written assignments, or as the basis for role-playing activities.

The role playing activities could be extended to a question not raised in the case: where should the headquarters of the new corporation be located? In relation to this question students could form groups representing the four different airline corporations and then play out the part of the national airline corporation during the negotiations of where to locate the headquarters.

The questions of the case touch upon international management (**Question 1**), and then moves on to some central themes in organisational behaviour: leadership, groups and motivation.

Guidance for answers

Question 1
The management of the new cross-cultural airline corporation?

In answering this question the work of Hofstede could be drawn upon. Hofstede found 4 dimensions upon which different cultures and their management behaviour vary:

1. Power Distance (PD)
2. Uncertainty Avoidance (UA)
3. Masculinity / Femininity (M/F)
4. Individualism / Collectivism (I/C).

How do the six countries fit into these dimensions?

Austria	PD LOW	UA strong	M	i
Denmark	PD LOW	UA WEAK	F	I
The Netherlands	PD low	UA weak	F	I
Norway	PD low	UA weak	F	i
Sweden	PD low	UA WEAK	F	I

20

Switzerland	PD low	UA strong	m	I

The use of capital letters indicates extreme values, e.g. UA WEAK means 'Very Weak' while UA weak means 'weak.'

There does not seem to be any big problems concerning Power Distance. All six countries are low on this dimension, although of varying degrees. The same goes for the Individualism/Collectivism dimension where all six countries are on the individual side.

Uncertainty Avoidance causes some problems. Both Austria and Switzerland are on the strong side while the other four countries are weak on this dimension. It seems that the best way to solve this is by keeping Uncertainty Avoidance weak. Such a compromise may be possible.

The Masculinity / Femininity dimension seems to present greater difficulties. The Scandinavian countries and Holland are very Feminine while Austria and Switzerland are on the Masculine side. It seems a big gap to bridge. It is important for the new management to make clear what is considered important and what is not, so that the employees will know what kind of behaviour is expected from them. The reward system in the company can be used to reinforce this by rewarding what is important (the expected behaviour).

Question 2

Carlzon used to be a charismatic leader. Why is he not seen in that way anymore?

> 'Charismatic leadership says that followers make attributions of heroic or extraordinary leadership abilities when they observe certain behaviors.' (Robbins, 1991, p. 379).

This applies to the situation Carlzon was in during and for some time after the economic turnaround of SAS in the early 80s.

Carlzon's lack of charismatic leadership now can be compared to the employee-centred or production-centred leader (Mullins, 1993).

In the 1980s Carlzon emphasised the employees and regarded them as the key to success. Due to the strategy of becoming one of the large airlines in Europe, Carlzon is today more concerned with the structure of the corporation and how SAS can be made one of the large airlines. This shift seems to go hand-in-hand with a shift in leadership-style from a democratic towards a more autocratic oriented style of leadership.

Carlzon is using a leadership-style with which the employees are dissatisfied. He has made mistakes. He might have been able to solve the situation when he was riding on a wave of success and sympathy. But that is no longer the case. The situation has changed and Carlzon is facing a wall of mistrust and disbelief. He might be doing the right thing, but even so he has lost his followers. His charisma has worn thin and the employees have little trust in him anymore. In short: what used to work for Carlzon now works against him.

Charismatic leaders often become victims of their own success. This might be what happened to Carlzon. The overwhelming self-confidence which charismatic leaders build up and possess can be the road to their own demise. It is difficult for charismatic leaders to listen to others and accept being challenged by their subordinates. They are convinced they are right. This might be the trap into which he has fallen. He no longer seems to be in tune with the employees, and his belief in being right has resulted in some costly mistakes.

Question 3

Should Carlzon get fired or should he stay?

Some reasons for removing Carlzon:

> Carlzon is discredited amongst the employees.

> Carlzon has made some costly mistakes.

> Carlzon will be a barrier in the negotiations with the employees.

> It could be argued that the situation of SAS now is changing, and that it, therefore, might be an appropriate opportunity to remove Carlzon. A change of senior management at SAS could signal that the company is now entering a new phase in joining the new corporation. At the same time this could be a signal to the employees that the company will appoint another person, who the employees trust, to represent SAS in the new corporation. In this way SAS might recapture the employees' trust.

Some reasons for keeping Carlzon as the managing director:

> He has had some success on the strategic side. It was his idea to focus on the businessman in the 1980s. Unfortunately, it was also Carlzon who was behind the purchase of shares in Intercontinental Hotels and Continental Airlines.

> Carlzon is a good negotiator and has played a major part in getting the corporation with KLM, Swissair, and Austrian Airlines started and kept on track.

Question 4

In the 80s SAS was 'one big happy family'. What has happened and how might this be

recaptured?

Today SAS is no longer united. The economic setback resulting in reductions in costs and staff has divided SAS. They are not working together to solve the problems, but against each other in order to pursue self-interest. This is clearly shown in the corporation's legal case against the employees for showing disloyal behaviour and the campaign by the employees which shows little faith in the leadership of SAS.

There seems to be a connection with the fact that the employees are no longer as involved in what is going on in SAS as they were during the economic turnaround in the 80's. This, of course, has to do with the fact that the decisions now being taken are more strategic than operational. The negotiations with other airlines make it hard to involve the employees in the decision making process. But this does not make the employees' frustrations any the less, they feel they are neither informed about nor involved in the decisions being made.

How can a united SAS be recaptured?

The possible removal of Carlzon is not enough, but it might be the signal that can start a process leading to a reunion between management and employees.

SAS should then emphasise that 'togetherness' will strengthen the position of SAS in the negotiations with the other parties and thereby increase the possibilities of making Copenhagen the headquartes of the new corporation. This would help motivation and reduce mistrust in management. At the same time it would allow employees to regain a degree of confidence in themselves.

The problem with this approach is that SAS is becoming united by turning the partners in the new corporation into enemies. This is not a good starting point for a healthy cooperation with the other airlines. If the new corporation is to succeed cooperation between the four airlines has to work.

Further reading

Ferraro, G. F. (1990). *The Cultural Dimension of International Business*, New Jersey: Prentice-Hall.

Joynt, P. and Warner, M. (1985). *Managing in Different Cultures*, Oslo: Universitetsforlaget.

Wilson, D. C. and Rosenfeld, R. H. (1990). *Managing Organisations*, Berkshire: McGraw-Hill.

Yukl, G. A. (1981). *Leadership in Organizations*, New Jersey: Prentice-Hall.

Case 6

MY GREATEST FAILURE: A CASE STUDY IN LEADERSHIP

Henner Hentze

How this case could be used

This case addresses one of the major themes of organizational leadership: namely the change from one style to another. The specific feature of the case is how national characteristics influence leadership style. Hence the case deals with both the theories of leadership and issues related to organisation development. The following learning points can be explored in this case:

- Analysis of leadership styles.
- The influence of national characteristics on the management of an enterprise.
- The relevance of organisational politics on leadership styles.

Readers may also gain an insight into how an organisation development project can be developed to manage a change of leadership styles.

How this case relates to theory

The issue of leadership is a key component of organisational behaviour. A number of theories have been developed which seek to explain what makes a 'good' leader and there is a growing body of evidence to suggest that the style of leadership is contingent upon the situation in which it is being practised. The most common variables cited are: environmental conditions, technology, the group to be lead and the task to be completed. In this case the key variable is the clash between French and German cultures. Hofstede's work has identified the relationship between leadership style and national cultures and the results of his research provide a useful starting point for an analysis of the issues raised by this case.

The case also touches on some socio-demographic characteristics of the workforce which can influence the process of communication and decision-making. The older employees in the French company identify strongly with the traditional organisation structure and its attributes. In order for them to adjust to a new leadership style there will be a need for training and education. As question 3 suggests such a change will require planned organisational development and the different models available can be explored in examining this case.

Guidance for answers

Question 1

Key points that may be considered here are:
- The highly centralised nature of French organisations, problems and communication

having to travel through the hierarchy, and the difficulties this gives in seeking a rapid response to change. The location of authority at the top of the organisation can be contrasted with the more co-operative German approach where delegation of authority and greater involvement of employees in the decision-making process is common.

- Werner's background and lack of detailed knowledge of the company's work has lead him to take a relatively passive approach to the management of production operations.
- Abel's style is characteristic of the manager who has learnt the job of a manager through experience. The 'patron' approach is consistent with the structure of French companies but means that all effective authority is concentrated in his hands. This produced a particular set of expectations amongst the workforce of the style of management to which they were exposed and resulted in a 'culture shock' when Bernard sought to introduce a very different style.
- Bernard's style is typical of German management, developed following the war, to encourage a more participative approach to management as an alternative to authoritarian structures previously in existence. Management by objectives, emphasising the cooperative element in determining job goals, is common in many German companies.
- The leadership problems result from Warner's lack of sensitivity to the changes taking place. There are significant differences between the amount of participation encouraged by Bernard and his predecessor and this has led to feelings of insecurity amongst the employees. For them, management by objectives appears to be seen as a sign of weakness in management.

A related question that may be considered is the extent to which these differences in leadership styles are solely due the nationalities of the managers concerned. Could similar problems arise in the approach of managers from the same culture?

Question 2

The decision on whether a different leadership style is appropriate for the company rests on M. Warner's assessment of pressures, particularly the social and technical ones, for change. Some aspects of these and their relation to the issues contained in the case are noted below.

Technological complexity and its increasing differentiation means that no one person can be an expert in all of its aspects. This implies a need to develop a team approach to the management of the company which can utilise the skills and knowledge of all members of in organization. It also suggests that the one-sided dependency characteristic of Abel's style will need to change. This will necessitate a change in the role of managers whose authority will stem from their ability to manage a team rather than from their formal position in the company.

The company may also face serious difficulties if it retains its current authoritarian structure. If all key decisions are taken by one manager any long term incapacity of that manager will have significant operational implications for the company.

The traditional work ethics of the ageing workforce are unlikely to be typical of the younger generation of employees. Their values are more likely to emphasis participation, involvement, self development and greater communication. Abel's style appears incompatible with these developments and if continued could give rise to problems for the organization in recruiting new employees. A management style similar to that offered by Bernard takes account of these societal changes and offers a more employee-orientated approach.

Question 3

If such changes are believed necessary then the process through which they are introduced will need to be carefully planned, a fact that was clearly not the case in the present situation. Had an assessment of the leadership style operating before Bernard's appointment be undertaken the resulting crisis may have been avoided or its effects limited. Similar difficulties are encountered when other organizational or technological innovations are made. This experience points to the need for a considered organisational development plan.

Dr Bernard needed the active support of Werner for the changes he planned to make. Employees would need to be convinced of the reasons for the change and how it could help secure the company's future. Equally Bernard should have been aware of the demands such an approach would have on his colleagues. Under Abel's leadership they had never been involved in the decision-making process. Participative styles of leadership have clear implications for such management issues such as delegation, goal definition and communication. A realistic timescale for the process should be set and progress monitored through regular feedback. An incremental approach might be recommended and the objectives of each phase met before the next is commenced. Changes to working practices should be complemented by formal training sessions and the value of using outside trainers considered.

Case 7

REALITY CATCHES UP WITH AUSSIECO

Robert Jones and Peter Gal

Question 1

Discuss the various issues of leadership raised by this case study.

Main points as a basis for discussion could include the following:

EVENT / INCIDENT	LEADERSHIP TRAIT
Owner has retained full control and ownership since 1962	Power Seeking
Most final decisions made by him	Mistrustful of ability of others
Mixed success in product diversification	Decisions made with inadequate objective research (gut feelings?)
Executive Managing Director is owner's nephew	Nepotistic appointments
Owner accepts order personally	Undermines his managers authority
Complaining Production Manager ordered out of his office	Refusal to listen to contradictory opinions
General Manager has no idea what is going on	Lack of communication

EVENT / INCIDENT	LEADERSHIP TRAIT
Owner 'deals with my people whenever he feels like it'	Ignores chain of command
Bonuses paid on whim of owner	Desire to retain control
Owner takes money out of company	Using company for own gratification
Limousine sports a bumper sticker	Divorced from reality

The performance of any organisation largely depends upon the leadership effectiveness and characteristics of the top person. The traits highlighted above indicate a domineering character, stubborn to the point of inflexibility, and with a belief in his own rightness and distrust of others which leads him to cling to control and power.

In terms of Behavioural Theory, his leadership style could be described as Authoritarian, or Boss-Centred in terms of the Tannenbaum and Schmidt Continuum ('manager makes decision and announces it'). The Ohio State Studies would indicate a style: high on Initiating Structure and low on Consideration; whilst Blake and Mouton Managerial Grid points to a 9,1 Authority — Obedience manager.

Question 2

Identify how the lack of managerial effectiveness has impacted upon the organisation

Mullins stresses the point that the majority of people come to work with the original intention of performing well. If performance fails to match this ideal this is largely a result of how staff perceive their treatment by management.

This case provides an example of how inappropriate leadership at the top of an organisation impacts upon managerial effectiveness and ultimately affects the performance of the entire organisation.

Managerial effectiveness must be related to the achievement of some purpose, objective or task. Since management involves getting work done through the co-ordinated efforts of other people, Mullins considers that effectiveness may be assessed, in part, therefore, by such factors as:

- Strength of motivation and morale of staff.
- Success of their training and development.
- Creation of an environment in which staff work willingly and effectively.

Discussion of the lack of managerial effectiveness through the above factors could be achieved by an examination of the following three elements: (a) failure to fulfil the traditional functions of management; (b) inappropriate organisational culture; (c) absence of employee commitment.

(a) <u>**Failure to fulfil the traditional functions of Management**</u>

ELEMENT OF MANAGEMENT	ADVERSE EVENTS / INCIDENTS
PLANNING	• Grooming inexperienced nephew to take over company • Ill-informed product and market diversification • Lack of knowledge of new markets • Redundant capacity in enlarged workshops
ORGANISING	• Stock out of resistors • Lack of inter-departmental communication • Incident of the forgotten welder • Frequency of personnel 'clangers'
DIRECTING	• Low morale and tardy behaviour of operatives • Lack of pride in the company • Prevalence of a fear factor • Ridicule of work measurement by employees
CONTROLLING	• Emphasis on production targets • Choosing suppliers on basis of cost • Insistence on employees clocking in and out

(b) <u>**Inappropriate organisational culture**</u>

Managerial failure to fulfil traditional functions, in turn moulds the type of

30

culture prevalent in the organisation. Discussion could revolve around the factors mentioned on p. 32 and 33.

CULTURE FACTOR	EVENTS/INCIDENTS
(i) What do managers consider important?	• Production targets • Time clocks • Following instructions • Cost minimisation
(ii) How do managers react to crises and critical events?	• Non performing employees are sacked • Rapid turnover of Production Managers (scapegoats?) • Complaining Production Manager ordered out of owner's office • Reorganisation of Programming Department (reactive management?) • Fear of relaying unpopular messages to owner
(iii) What role models are provided by managers?	• Separate dining room • Access to alcohol (denied to employees) • Arrive for work between 9.00 and 10.00am • Playing golf • General Manager 'kicks around' other managers
(iv) What are the criteria for distributing rewards?	• Bonuses paid on whim of owner • No internal promotions • Rewards flow to the top

(v)	What are the criteria for hiring and firing	• Unqualified migrants at operative level • Nepotism and favouritism in hiring • Non-performing workers are sacked

(c) <u>**Absence of Employee Commitment**</u>

In turn the lack of a positive culture at Aussie Co. impacts upon the commitment of employees.

Discussion could revolve around the following three-pillar model of commitment (following Martin and Nicholls (1987), *Creating a committed workforce*, London: IPS).

PILLAR OF EMPLOYEE COMMITMENT	ADVERSE EVENTS/INCIDENTS
Sense of Belonging ♦ Informed ♦ Involved ♦ Sharing in Success	• Orders are sent from top to bottom • Ideas and personal opinions are neither sought nor valued • Deception of the senior programmer • Process worker fired for complaining • Refusal of company to supply references • Little or no money budgeted for training
Sense of Excitement ♦ Pride ♦ Trust ♦ Accountability for Results	• Staff move slowly to their positions • Assembly line workers hold back production with weak and vague excuses • 100 metre dash from the premises • Very few employees used the bumper stickers

PILLAR OF EMPLOYEE COMMITMENT	ADVERSE EVENTS/INCIDENTS
Confidence in Management ◆　　Authority ◆　　Dedication ◆　　Competence	• Ineffectiveness of GM's post-lunch tour • Nobody knows who the GM is • Employment of unqualified Production Supervisor (jobs for mates?) • Management concentrate on short-term financial survival

Other points for discussion

Tutors may also find it useful to discuss the following characteristics of AussieCo:

- The prevalence of a Theory X approach to human nature. (Students could be asked to identify those incidents/events in the case which support this contention.)
- The employment of Scientific Management principles. (Students could be asked to identify those incidents/events in the case which support this contention.)
- The tendency to Likert's System 1 organisational characteristics (Exploitative/Authoritative). Students could be requested to complete the Short Form Profile of Organisational Characteristics. By answering the various questions relating to the organisational variables of Leadership, Motivation, Communication, Decisions, Goals and Control, they should be able to verify the System 1 nature of the organisation.

Further reading

Students who wish to pursue further reading of the organisational behavioural characteristics inherent in 'excellent' companies are referred to any of the books below.

Crosby, P.B. (1992). *The Eternally Successful Organisation*, Mentor.

Goldsmith, W. and Clutterbuck, D. (1984). *The Winning Streak*, Harmondsworth: Penguin.

Peters, T.J. and Waterman, R.H. JR (1982). *In Search of Excellence*, New York: Harper and Row.

For further reading on the characteristics of effective managers, students are referred to the popular and easy-to-read text below.

Freemantle, D. (1990). *Incredible Bosses*, Maidenhead: McGraw-Hill.

Case 8

THAMESIDE: LEADERSHIP WITHIN A LOCAL AUTHORITY HOUSING DEPARTMENT

Sarah L. Henson and Fred Turner

How the case can be used

There are many ways of analysing the issue of leadership. This case aims to provide the student with an opportunity to explore the link between theoretical issues and practice by relating the topic of leadership and management to the context of a public sector organisation.

The case study draws attention to a wide range of organisational behaviour issues as a basis for discussion and analysis. In particular, it allows students to critically evaluate from a number of perspectives many of the problems and difficulties faced for effective leadership. The answers to the questions posed by the activity brief are by no means conclusive, but are to be used as a basis for enquiry and exploration.

The objectives of this case are:

- To provide an integrated view of leadership.

- To develop and enhance the link between both theoretical and practical issues relating to leadership.

- To demonstrate an awareness of the characteristics of leadership in private and public sector organisations.

- To identify the influence of situational factors on the effectiveness of leadership in work organisations.

- To improve knowledge and skills necessary for developing problem solving abilities.

Guidance for answers

Question 1

What do you understand by the term leadership?

This is particularly appropriate for stimulating a discussion on leadership within work organisations. An understanding of the various theoretical contributions to the nature of leadership could be explored, allowing students to understand clearly the context in which the term is used and how leadership theories have evolved and been modified.

Alternatively, students will be able to address the relationship between leadership and the concept of management, highlighting both their similarities and differences.

In answering this particular question, a number of organisational behaviour texts detail the issue and topic of leadership. Mullins (1993) and Handy (1993) (Recommended Reading) both provide a useful summative guide to leadership. The latter offers an invaluable overview to further reading on this subject.

Question 2 and 2.1

What conclusions do you draw concerning the effectiveness of Michael's leadership? To what extent is the leader-follower relationship affected by situational factors?

Whilst the case points to an exploration of a number of differing issues and concepts in organisational behaviour, it confronts primarily the experiences of one local government officer. (However, this might serve as an example for other individual work experiences within this type of organisation.)

In attempting to outline the events and circumstances within the organisation, these questions bring into question the ability and effectiveness of Michael's leadership as well as highlighting the importance of what we might consider and interpret to be effective leadership and how we would measure and record this.

Furthermore, the questions provide students with the opportunity to assess and explore those factors which affect the basis of the leader—follower relationship. In particular, factors such as an appreciation of some of the following variables: the skills and attributes of the individual, characteristics of the subordinates, the relationship between the manager and the group, the nature of the organisation, the influence of both external and internal policies and procedures, organisational culture, the nature of the tasks to be achieved, nature of the decisions to be taken and finally although not conclusively, the role of power and politics at work.

Suitable material covering the issues here, can be found in the recommended reading to this case. For a more critical account refer to Thompson and McHugh (1990).

Question 3

Critically discuss the conflicts of interest evident in this case. To what do you attribute them?

This assignment could be used as a basis for understanding the essence of the problems and difficulties posed for effective leadership within this local authority context, by way of examining and exploring the nature of the officer—elected member relationship.

It will also stimulate an awareness of how role conflict, power and influence, communication, and inter-group behaviour provide barriers for effective leadership. An appreciation of organisational culture and the importance of norms and their influence upon individual commitment and behaviour will focus on the management of the officer—elected member relationship.

These themes will demonstrate how the leadership—follower relationship is constrained in this local authority and how informal systems and individual objectives can interfere with the smooth operation of a department.

A useful account of the role and influence of power in work organisations can be found in Wilson and Rosenfeld (1990). For a more critical introduction to the issues relating to this particular question see Thompson and McHugh (1990).

Question 4

How might leadership and management differ, if at all, within public and private sector organisations? Give your reasons.

This discussion should help demonstrate that although private sector and public organisations have a large degree of commonality in the way they are led and managed, there does exist some fundamental differences between the two sectors.

This question aims to stimulate students awareness of the contextual problem of management and leadership in public sector organisations, despite Government attempts to assimilate their practices, in particular, how the process of leadership and management may face additional operational difficulties due to the nature of the organisation.

Similarity between the two sectors might be evident in: characteristics of the leader, tasks to be achieved, the role of power at work, characteristics of the subordinates, decisions to be taken and organisational change. Whilst differences in the public sector could include: emphasis on 'professional' standards, the emphasis on service to the local community, internal and external influences and procedures, management systems and policy co-ordination, accountability and responsibility to the local community, constraints on public spending, politically motivated objectives, legal and political dimensions and traditional rights to staff tenure.

For a more extensive account of public sector administration see Greenwood and Wilson (1989) (Recommended Reading) and Johnson (1983).

Question 5

What recommendations or further action could be taken to overcome some of the

leadership difficulties you have identified in this case.

This question is suitable for developing students analytical skills, by providing them with the opportunity to reflect and prepare a number of possible remedies to this case.

Consideration of the events and outcomes of the case taken from a number of different perspectives will allow students to appreciate all the factors inherent in this organisation which have contributed towards the goal of effective leadership.

With careful analysis, a number of recommendations or further action could be taken to effectively match both individual and organisational needs. Organisational strategies which could form a basis for further action might include: improvements to organisational induction programmes, improved staff training and development, remedies to effective communication, greater clarity of work roles and individual expectations, techniques for dealing with organisational change, better co-ordination of organisational workloads and more effective delegation.

The references used previously will provide suitable material for answering this question.

Further reading

Johnson. N. (1993). 'Management in Government' in Earl M.J. (Ed.), *Perspectives on Management: A Multidisciplinary Analysis*, London: Oxford University Press.

Thompson. P. and McHugh. D. (1990). *Work Organisations: A Critical Introduction*, London: Macmillan.

Wilson D.C. and Rosenfeld R.H. (1990). *Managing Organizations: Text, Readings and Cases*, UK: McGraw-Hill International .

Part 3
Context of the Organisation

Case 9

OTICON — SPAGHETTI FOR THE EARS

Pernille Eskerod and Per Darmer

The case highlights some important aspects of the change process (especially that of resistance to change) and looks more closely and critically at organisational structure. The case with its questions is primarily designed as a basis for group discussion but it can be used as a written assignment.

Guidance for answers

Question 1

The reasons behind the success of Oticon in minimizing resistance to change?

The key may be full involvement of employees and allowing them have a say in the restructuring of the company. This led to increased motivation and commitment to the change process.

Specific action taken by the company included:

- Openness about the restructuring and its consequences.

- Oticon took time (three years) and made the proper preparation. Management and employees discussed means and ends and the consequences for the employees to lessen insecurity amongst employees.

- All employees attended a meeting before the restructuring actually took place to get the latest information, to have the opportunity to pose questions and get misunderstandings out of the way.

- The employees were allowed to take a PC home before the change was launched. In this way the employees could become familiar with the PC and get rid of whatever fear they might have had for such 'machinery'.

Question 2

The organisational structure of Oticon?

Organisational structure consists of three dimensions (Robbins, 1991) and these, together with their application to Oticon, are shown below:

1. Complexity: Low
   (a) Horizontal differentiation: Low
       - The Departments have been abolished.
       - Reduced specialisation. Project participation provides employees with, and also uses more general skills.

43

(b)   Vertical differentation: Low
-        Oticon has a very flat hierarchy. The project managers report direct to senior management.

(c)   Spatial differentation: Medium to High

-        Oticon actually has factories in 10 different countries and a separate headquarters.

2.   Formalisation: Low

Oticon has very few rules and procedures. It aims to be flexible and innovative and this may be inconsistent with detailed rules and procedures.

3.   Centralisation: Low (decentralisation)

The project managers have some authority that they hardly ever use. Top management leaves most of the decision making to the employees; only decision top management seems to make concerns the acceptance of projects.

Mintzberg's 1983 theory of organisational structure is both well-known and widespread. But it seems that Oticon does not fit neatly into any of Mintzberg's 1983 five configurations or organisational designs.

Oticon is **not** a matrix-organisation. It has project-groups, but Oticon has no departments and has become a pure project-organisation.

By closely considering Mintzberg's five configurations it seems that the configuration which Oticon most resembles is the professional bureaucracy. It is the professionals who make up the project-groups: the key element in Oticon. This is underlined by putting the individual at the centre in order that the individual's creativity can be utilised to develop new products and provide the high levels of service desired. Still this configuration is not fully matched by with Oticon. The company is low on complexity whereas the professional bureaucracy is high on this dimension. In the professional bureaucracy the operating core is the specialists with standardised skills that have been internalised through their professionalism. In Oticon they are no longer professionals in the same sense as true to their profession, but rather team-players on projects.

If Oticon — or Oticon look-alikes — is the organisational structure of the future then consideration will need to be given to Mintzberg's configurations being extended to include one new configuration or design that seems to fit projects - based organisations like Oticon.

Question 3

Advantages and disadvantages of Oticon's spaghetti-organisation?

The following list highlights the most important advantages and disadvantages of Oticon's project-organisation. The lists have been compiled by the authors following interviews with employees. It should be stressed that almost every single item on the lists has two sides, which means that most of the advantages bring along some kind of disadvantage.

Advantages:

- A flexible and adaptive organisation.

- Promotes productivity and innovation.

- Self-responsibility, autonomy, trust in people and participation, which helps to bring out creative forces in staff.

- Decentralisation in form of a flat democratic structure pointing in the direction of equality.

- The flat structure and the informal communication cause information to flow much faster.

- A more holistic view of the company (gained by participating in different projects at the same time and over time).

- Using more of employees' abilities than just their specific professional skills.

- Administration is kept at a low level.

Disadvantages:

- The projects can narrow the minds of the employees to the project on which they are working and fighting for, rather than to the company as a whole. (Suboptimization)

- Problems with coordinating all the projects which might very easily result in confusion and 'double-jobbing' (a reverse synergy effect).

- Those performing the necessary routine tasks which have to be done are very low in status.

- Demoraliising effect on the employees when their projects are abandoned.

- Competition amongst employees for membership of the better projects can create a segmentation in the organisation between those who are successful (and therefore will be in demand for other promising projects) and those of the employees who are not and, therefore, will be in low demand for future projects.
- People preferring structured jobs are uncomfortable in the flexible and innovative world of Oticon.

- The open plan office leaves very little privacy for the individual employee to perform demanding tasks in peace and quiet. At the same time this arrangement provides scope for pressure and control of the employee by leaders and peers. This might lead to high levels of stress.

- Shifting workplace, colleagues, and tasks also promote a high level of stress.

- The employees become 'Oticon generalists' which might limit opportunities for jobs outside the company. It also takes time to make new employees into 'Oticon generalists'.

Question 4

How to eliminate/minimize the disadvantages of Oticon's spaghetti-organisation?

Oticon has not yet solved these problems themselves. Those that might be considered are:-

- The coordination in Oticon might be improved through meetings between the project-leaders. The meeting ought to reflect Oticon's ideas of democracy, informal and open communication in a flat structure where the leaders do not use their formal authority. Such a step would be in accordance with the company's emphasis on face-to-face communication.

- It is very hard to upgrade routine tasks in a project-organisation where they are considered a necessary evil. Oticon tries to solve it through rotation of these routine tasks. An alternative solution might be to let some of the employees who prefer structured jobs take over these tasks.

- Competition is part of the Oticon culture, but a more structured approach to group membership selection might lessen the damage that this can cause. It might also be that the project-leaders if they regularly work the same group of employees in all the projects might not recognise the danger of group — think limiting their groups creativity.

FINDING YOUR WAY: USING ACTION RESEARCH AND COGNITIVE MAPPING METHODS IN STRATEGY FORMULATION

K Alan Rutter

The case concerns a firm seeking a new strategic direction in an environment that is highly uncertain and turbulent. It describes how new methods of strategy formulation were used by a researcher to enable the managers of the firm to explore their perception of their firm's environment and to identify a strategy which they felt they 'owned'.

The case study is based on recent research in the field of strategic management which builds on personal and social construct theories to explore the influence of individual and group perceptions of their world and how these influence strategy formulation. Based on the precept that personal boundaries or frameworks can inhibit active search for new understanding and meaning, methods must be employed which challenge people's beliefs in order to bring about creative management. In this case study, action research methods were used to reveal these frameworks and cognitive mapping was used to capture and explicate them.

The case can be used on undergraduate courses as an example of environmental scanning in strategic management, or as an illustration of individual and team organizational behaviour issues. It can also be used as an integrated strategic management/organizational behaviour/research methodology case on MBA courses.

Question 1

This question focuses on how people 'see' their enacted environment and how this perception can be revealed and challenged through the use of cognitive maps.

The first meeting with the managers was an unstructured, free-flowing conversation around what the managers saw 'out there'. The topics that came up were frequently categorized by the team as 'threats' or 'opportunities'. The team agreed that these two categories would be a good starting point for the more structured sessions that were to follow. It might be of interest to ask the students to discuss the two lists of 'threats' and 'opportunities'. For instance, to what extent are the topics listed environmental factors in the strategic management sense?

The 'Threat' Map

The map suggests that Attle Marine is under capitalised and is being squeezed very hard on margins. This was, in fact, the case, but the seriousness of the financial situation was only known by Toby and, possibly, Sylvia.

It also suggests that there is a tension between the need to go for high volume smaller boats or to specialise in high margin low volume boats, especially ones for the government.

The 'Opportunity' Map

Although the session which produced this map was focused on possible new strategic directions for the firm, a number of constraints were expressed which tempered enthusiasm that might have arisen for any suggested new opportunity. For instance, financial and overhead constraints ('Fin.' and O/Hs' on the map) to developing commercial boats came by the team. The session made the team realise that in order for the firm to move into a new market and industry either they recruited a specialist in that field, or one of them had to drop some of his or her current work load to concentrate on bringing in new business from their chosen business area.

The firm's strategic decision

These strategic management sessions led Toby to have a separate meeting with Howard, and together they set up a separate unit called Attle Commercial Boats. Jason was left to continue selling the leisure boats. David was not consulted by Toby after these sessions were over, since Toby believed that David was incapable of obtaining a managerial perspective on running a factory.

The new unit had its own identity and publicity material, but did not have any assets of its own. Sylvia was instrumental in creating the promotional campaign and organizing the production of a video to promote the new operation. Under its new identity, the unit tendered for and won a major new contract from the British government. Shortly after winning this contract, Toby sold the firm to a large publicly quoted company with interests in marine engineering. As part of the transfer of ownership package, Toby became the managing director of the holding company and reported directly to the chairman.

Both Sylvia and Howard were excited and motivated by the changes. Jason preferred to reserve judgement since his position became that of 'merely one of the sales team reporting to a sales director' in the larger organization. David was very dissatisfied with the outcome for two reasons. Firstly, his 'presence' was reduced. He is responsible for the smallest manufacturing plant in the company and now reported to a manufacturing director at Head Office instead of Toby. Secondly, he felt that it is difficult for him to find anyone in the organisation who will listen to his problems.

Question 2

Action research methodology is used extensively in the fields of education, criminology, psychotherapy and other areas of social science research. The method is useful when working with people who need practical assistance in making changes. However, from the stand-point of traditional scientific research the method's greatest weakness lies in the difficulty of validating the findings.

The students might like to address the questions put forward by Gareth Morgan in his book *Imagination* (1993):

1.   How can the researcher understand what is happening in the sessions?

2.   How can the researcher validate her interpretation as she goes along?

3.   How can the researcher present his insights in a constructive manner at the sessions?

4.   How can the researcher realise her mandate that is ethical and that respects the competing interests and ideas that can be generalised from the situation to others?

5.   What can the researcher and others learn from the project in which he is engaged?

Cognitive maps were used to capture the managers' enacted environment. These maps are metaphors of the managers' 'reality' and therefore need to be accurate reflections of their perceptions. The students could discuss the strengths and weaknesses of the method, particularly the interpretation the researcher will put on the data gleaned from the tape-recorded transcripts. How did the researcher in the case tackle this problem? What other steps could the researcher have taken to make certain that the strategic solution that the team come up with is 'owned' by them and that the researcher's influence was reduced?

Question 3

The researcher in the case was not entirely convinced that Toby was levelling with him. He felt that the strategic direction had already been decided by Toby, and that he was using the sessions to promote his point of view and to prepare the others for what he had already decided.

Since Toby was the sole owner of the business, it could be argued that he was perfectly entitled to make whatever decision he chose. It is not clear whether Toby made his decision as a consequence of the sessions or whether he made them before. Nevertheless, some of the team members felt alienated and the question remains as to whether a genuine collegiate approach would have been more beneficial.

Against these factors the case provides an opportunity to examine issues related to group working and group leadership. In particular, the effectiveness of group decision making and communication, and the impact upon group processes of such issues as 'group think', can be explored.

Further reading

Berger, P. l. and Luckmann, T. (1976). *The Social Construction of Reality*, Harmondsworth, England: Penguin.

Chakravarthy, B. S. and Doz, Y. (1992). 'Strategy process research: focusing on corporate self-renewal', *Strategic Management Journal*, 13, pp. 5—14.

Eden, C. (1992). 'On the Nature of Cognitive Maps', *Journal of Management Studies*, 29, pp. 261—265.

Eden, C. and Ackermann, S. (1992). 'The analysis of cause maps', *Journal of Management Studies*, 29, pp. 309—324.

Fiol, C. M. and Huff, A. S. (1992), 'Maps for Managers: Where are we? Where do we go from here?', *Journal of Management Studies*, 29, pp. 267—285.

Jackson, S. E. and Dutton, J. E. (1988). 'Discerning Threats and Opportunities', *Administrative Science Quarterly*, 33, pp. 370—387.

Lenz, R. T. and Engledow, J. L. (1986). 'Environmental analysis: The applicability of current theory', *Strategic Management Journal*, 7, pp. 329—346.

Smircich, L. and Stubbart, C. (1985). 'Strategic Management in an Enacted Way', *Academy of Management Review*, 10, pp. 724—736.

Stubbart, C. I. (1989). 'Managerial cognition: a missing link in strategic management research', *Journal of Management Studies*, 26, pp. 325—347.

Weick, K. E. 'Cartographic Myths in Organizations', in Huff, A. S. (Ed.), (1990). *Mapping Strategic Thought*, Chichester, England: John Wiley.

Case 11

LEISUREDROME PLC - ACQUISITION OF ASSETS OR LIABILITIES?

Karen Meudell

Question 1

Using the concepts of organisation structure evaluate LEL's approach to its restructuring of the organisation following the acquisition of Sundance.

The main issue for the Company is that it was felt that the introduction of functional support staff and the introduction of 'loyal' LEL managers into the two new Regional Offices would prove to be the ultimate panacea and would solve any problems which might have been anticipated.

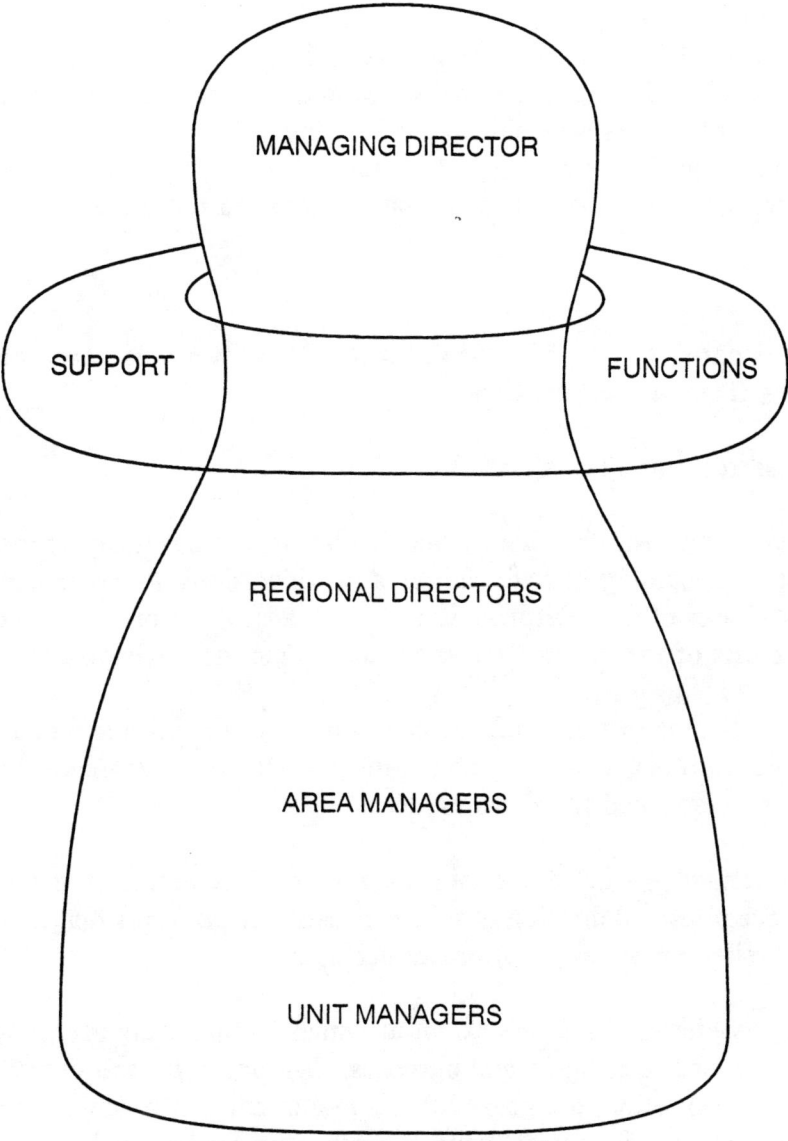

Fig. 11.1   Adapted from Mintzberg, H. (1983) Structure in Fires: *Desiging Effective Organisations*, Englewood Cliffs, Prentice Hall

There were, however, in reality, two main issues: the mechanistic one of structural design to suit the new organisational requirements and the behavioural issue associated with the acquisition. In practice a mechanistic approach was taken: no thought was given to the long term implications of the restructuring; no attempt was made to monitor the changes and the main emphasis was placed on the 'engineering' issues, publicity and PR. Whilst laudable attention was given, with very good reason, to the integration of Sundance staff, the manner in which it was carried out only served to emphasise the 'them and us' attitude.

Given that the pre-acquisition culture of LEL resembled Handy's (1993) Web/Power culture (i.e. few rules and procedures with communication depending largely on personal conversation), an alternative approach which could have been taken would have been to harness this culture with the Managing Director as the central figure, by the introduction of an adaptation of Mintzberg's Simple Structure with professional support as a 'collar'. This is illustrated in Figure 11.1.

This would have ensured that control was exercised centrally, that the organisation was strong and could react quickly to threat. Additionally it would have provided an integrated approach where Unit and Area Managers were able to contract and report to whichever support function they felt in need of. Equally, by keeping to a minimum the activities under the control of the Managing Director, he would have ensured that the web did not break.

Question 2

Considering the expansion from 15 to 51 units at LEL, how would you manage the issues of control arising from the acquisition?

The following research could be referred to:

(a)   Sloan (1965) suggests that whilst decentralisation is necessary to prevent regional management becoming stifled and to allow decisions to be made closer to the operational bases of the enterprise, it may also cause decisions to be made with regard to the interests of the region concerned rather than the Division as a whole.

(b)   Etzioni (1971) puts forward the idea that in order to establish and maintain control in an organisation it is necessary to obtain the compliance of its members. He proposes that this be approached from two aspects:

     (i)   'structural' — i.e. the establishment of a hierarchy of authority, specified procedures and division of labour because he contends that individuals cannot be relied on to carry out orders perfectly.

     (ii)   'motivational' — i.e. the extent to which the members of the organisation are committed to its aims and purposes. The more the individual is involved in the organisation, the greater the commitment to the achievement of its goals and the need for formal control mechanisms is lessened.

Post-acquisition, LEL displayed examples of both (i) and (ii) above. All three regions were making decisions for the benefit of themselves rather than the Division as a whole. Further, although there existed, on paper, a hierarchy of authority, it was impossible to expect the commitment of individuals to organisational aims since these had never been truly defined and the compensating control mechanisms were non-existent.

Sloan suggests that there is a need for what he terms 'co-ordinated decentralisation' and this was clearly not considered in the Sundance acquisition. Too great an emphasis was placed on growth, market leadership and the individual kudos which would result from attaining this and too little thought was given to the organisational and behavioural problems that this would cause.

The issue could have been addressed by considering the restructuring discussed in (1) above.

Further reading

Etzioni, A. (1971). *A Comparative Analysis of Complex Organisations*, New York: Free Press.

Handy, C. (1993). *Understanding Organisations*, London: Penguin.

Sloan, A. P. (1965). *My Years with General Motors*, Sidgwick and Jackson.

Case 12

THE CHALLENGE OF OBTAINING VALUE FOR MONEY IN PRESCRIBING IN THE NATIONAL HEALTH SERVICE

Jeff Watling

How the case can be used

As indicated in the 'Introduction' to this case it is likely to be of particular interest to those working in the public sector, especially managers working in the NHS. This problem is so complex that simply tinkering with a single dimension such as structure or introducing draconian controls simply will not do. The NHS is publicly accountable and the government of the day is accountable to the public for the NHS, so measures introduced by managers must be demonstrably reasonable in the eyes of the public and government. Students will benefit from trying to identify ways forward which will achieve their objectives but allow others to benefit also.

It is recommended that the McKinsey 7-S framework highlighted in Chapter 21 of Mullins (1993) is used to review this case study.

Relation to the Model

The model is valuable for analysing the case, particulary, if the 7-S headings are expanded to clarify their meaning. For example if one looks at the situation prior the Purchaser/ Provider Split:

STRUCTURE

Organisation — accountability.
How tasks are integrated into the organisation.

Students should identify that the problem here is not so much the structure (Figure 1. illustrates the pre - Purchaser/provider split organisational structure of the NHS), as the accountability of the doctors, particularly for their prescribing practice.

SHARED VALUES

What the organisation stands for.
How the organisation behaves in tough times.

Students should identify the Shared values of the NHS which from a prescribing perspective are to allow clinical freedom. This is further emphasised by the crisis behaviour which has been adopted over the years.

SYSTEMS

The formal and informal processes within the organisation - systems for:

- **accounting**
- **quality assurance**
- **performance measurement**

Students should identify the systems for controlling expenditure on medicines:

- Hospital formularies, but what are their shortcomings?
- Guidelines for treatment of common diseases, but what are their limitations?
- Drug and therapeutics committees to advise on the prescribing and administration of medicines, but where do they fit in the structure?

Similarly students should identify the systems for evaluating new medicines and their shortcomings:

- clinical trials;
- the Regional Development and Evaluation Committee;
- making cases for new products;
- potential benefits of research and development

SKILLS

The collective skills of the organisation.
What the organisation is good at.

Students should identify that collective skills of the NHS organisation are directed towards applying downward pressure on historically based budgets and not on evaluating and making the best use of the available resources. The NHS is poor at looking at the global resource and employing it flexibly.

STAFF

Their demographics, experience, education and training.
The fit between jobs and what needs to be done.

Students should identify the shortcomings of post graduate medical and pharmaceutical education and training. In particular the fact that it is not directed towards.

- cost benefit analysis
- health economics
- pharmacoeconomics
- drug use evaluation

STRATEGY

Plans for allocation of resources.

Students should identify the tendency to:

- allocate resources on previous year's budgets regardless of workload or change in practice;
- under-fund developments.

Whilst recognising that some good practice is emerging in the primary care sector.

STYLE/SYMBOLIC BEHAVIOUR

What managers consider important.
What managers spend time on.
The results they reward.
The way they act in a crisis.

Students should identify where managers were going wrong:

- not spending enough time on budget setting and controlling expenditure;
- bailing out overspenders.

A similar approach should be adopted for 'Proposals for the Future'.

Guidance on answers to the questions set at the end of the case

Question 1

Analysis of the situation

This question is not intended to be answered and work submitted for marking. It does however form a basis for answering **Questions 2—4**. A brainstorming technique involving each of the 7-S headings in turn, looking first at issues in the past and then at current and future issues, will give a clear guide, in particular, to the cultural, structural and systems problems of the past and how they can be overcome in the future.

Question 2

The paper for the GMT

The paper should be relatively short, 1000—1500 words. The RHA should only suggest strategies for the introduction of change and then hold Purchasers to account for implementing them. The purchaser/provider split has created real opportunities for the future. The creation of the Health Commissions has created a unique opportunity because of the dual interest of the Health Commissions in primary and secondary care. The framework should be used to identify these opportunities and exploit them. In particular the following issues should be emphasised:

STRUCTURE

Students will need to recognise that the changes in structure (see Figure 2.) has defined the accountability of the consultant in the hospital service. The NHS Trusts, in turn, are clearly accountable to their customers through the contracts process.

SYSTEMS

Students should identify that systems should be introduced for:

Evaluation of new medicines

The development and evaluation committee is the first step towards rational control of the introduction of new medicines. However, the rate of development will always outstrip the availability of funds for developments. Bochner (1992) describes a system introduced in the Royal Adelaide Hospital. The goal of the system was to provide a ranking of drug requests on the basis of obtaining the greatest benefit for each dollar spent.

The following controls should apply to the hospital service:

- Formularies that apply to everyone, including consultants.
- Systems for introduction of new medicines which ensure funding before change of practice.
- D and Th Committees strengthened to take on a role associated with budget setting and control.
- D and Th committees to be firmly locked into the management structure.
- Improved budget setting based on workload.
- Specific service agreements to be set up which describe the nature of care on offer.

The following controls should apply to primary care:

- general implementation mechanisms for:
    - promoting generic prescribing;
    - promoting guidelines for treatment of disease.

- GPs should be encouraged to go through the educational process of jointly developing a practice formulary by negotiation with their own partners.

- GPs should have to obtain approval and funding before they prescribe new medicines in the same way as proposed for hospital consultants.

Quality assurance and audit

- Management should switch emphasis of research and development strategy and audit towards:

    - cost benefit analysis ;
    - health economics ;
    - pharmacoeconomics (see also skills below).

57

STRATEGY

Students should emphasise the fact that managers should use all seven components of the framework to introduce change. RHA Directors should behave in such a way as to make it clear to the Organisation that they intend to change the culture of the organisation by working together and using the new structures to develop: systems, organisational skills and staff to demonstrate that they intend to obtain value for money from prescribed medicines.

Once this is established and agreed they will need to ensure that Trusts and other providers (including GPs) have systems in place to:

(a)   control expenditure on existing medicines and
(b)   control the introduction and use of new medicines as they are developed.

Question 3

The paper for the Regional Medical Advisory Committee.

Emphasis will need to be placed very strongly on quality and making the best use of resources. The Regional Medical Advisory Committee will be reluctant to endorse any measures which will be seen by their colleagues to restrict the right of individuals to prescribe what is best for their patients.

Students should use all the levers from the framework to persuade members of the committee that there is need for change and how it should be implemented. In particular the students should concentrate on the following:

STYLE

Students should recognise the role of management in:

Budget setting

If management is to gain any credibility in this area more time and effort will have to be put into the budget setting process.

Accountability

Once budget setting has been improved it would be reasonable to delegate budgets to clinicians and expect them to manage within them. Rewards/sanctions should also be evaluated.

STAFF

Students should recognise the importance of switching the emphasis of post graduate education and training for doctors and pharmacists to:

- cost benefit analysis,
- health economics and
- pharmacoeconomics.

This together with the change of emphasis in research and development and audit strategies will enhance the skills of the organisation towards obtaining better value for money in prescribing.

SHARED VALUES

Students should emphasise the need to change the culture of the organisation. In particular managements should change their behaviour in the following areas:

- setting realistic medicines budgets;
- introducing simple systems for evaluating the benefits of new medicines and prioritising them;
- investing in the right sort of education for doctors, pharmacists and nurses in cases where they are prescribers;
- involvement of prescribers in all stages of the process.

Question 4

The human resources and training issues associated with this case.

It is important to enlist the support of existing training agencies and redirect their activities rather than trying to set up new systems. In general, control frameworks encouraging local initiatives should be encouraged. Whilst there is a temptation to concentrate on the high cost prescribers both in hospitals and general practice, it is also important to realise that the *'silent majority'* will make larger overall savings by a relatively small shift in practice than the top 10% who could reduce their costs by 20-30%, but will fight every inch of the way. The most important groups to influence are clearly the prescribers of the future, so that undergraduates and newly qualified hospital doctors and GP trainees should all be encouraged to evaluate what they are doing and make the best use of resources available. In addition to doctors, it must be remembered that many other health care workers influence prescribing practice. Nurse, particularly those working in the community and primary care sectors should be considered together with pharmacists, dieticians and physiotherapists.

MIDDLE MANAGEMENT EXPERIENCES OF DEVOLUTION IN BARSETSHIRE COUNTY COUNCIL SOCIAL SERVICES DEPARTMENT

Linda Keen

The main objective of this case study is to enable students to become aware of the problematic reality of organisational structure and behaviour — hence the extensive use of middle managers' own views — and to be able to make sense of it in terms of the theoretical models available in the mainstream literature, mainly Mintzberg in this case although other texts on the forms of organisation structure can be utilised.

Question 1

Students should be able to place many of the changes described in the study within the context of Mintzberg's design parameters, outlined briefly in his 1989 text, but much more thoroughly in the 1983 text, with a useful diagram on pages 280—281. A particularly interesting point here relates to the basis of the unit groupings — from the combined market/product and functions grouping characteristics of traditional professional organisations (such as the Barset SSD) to the Purchaser/Provider split within each SSD Area on the basis of function. From the design parameters, it is a natural progression to consider BCC within the context of the machine and professional bureaucracies and the divisionalised/diversified forms.

Question 2

Students need to differentiate clearly between the terms frequently used in the quotations - accountability, responsibility, authority, power etc. Mintzberg's definition of decentralisation, in terms of horizontal and vertical types of decentralisation, is extremely useful here, as is also his continuum of control over the decision making process — see Chapter 5 in the 1983 text. Mintzberg's idea of the competing 'pulls' on the organisation is relevant here, together with the problems controlling the devolved management units, and hence, the tendencies towards bureaucratization; there are numerous examples of various procedural mechanisms represented in the quotations, together with, of course, moves towards coordination through the performance appraisal and business planning system, and through a coherent organisation culture. See Chapters 6 and 9 in the 1989 text.

Question 3

This study focuses on changes in the manager's decisional roles, but clearly there will be impacts, which the students can be invited to consider, on the interpersonal and information roles — see Mintzberg's 1973 text for detail, and the 1989 text for a summary. The problematic position of middle managers centres around the paradox of what Smith calls 'coercive autonomy', the frustrations of requirements to become more autonomous and accountable, while subjected simultaneously to more rigorous organisation control. See Stewart (1991), Chapters 9 and 10, and Scase (1989) for the implications of devolution for managers' work roles, work satisfaction, work pressures, career progression, new competencies required etc., some of which are mentioned in the study. The utility of the concept of 'role' — organised sets of behaviour associated with a particular position — for analysing managerial work can be discussed, in terms of formal role demands from the organisation on managerial jobs, differentiated by their particular function and hierarchical position, and the managers' own role expectations and perceptions. See Hales' (1993) article and Stewart (1991), Chapters 3 and 4.

Question 4

Students should apply Mintzberg's consistency factors (see the 1989 text, Chapter 6) to local government. Key issues here include the highly political nature of some difficult-to-measure non-routined activities (like social work), which, because of the principle of democratic accountability, require public justification in terms of both means and ends. Unlike the private sector, local government is not concerned with demand by "customers" for products at a price in the market, nor can it, generally, generate income from the market, depending largely on central government for funding. There is also increasing regulation of activities through Government and EC legislation.

Further reading

For a fuller account of Mintzberg's models of organisational structures and managerial roles, see:

Mintzberg, H. (1973). *The Nature of Managerial Work*, New Jersey: Prentice Hall.

Mintzberg, H. (1983). *Structure in Fives*, New Jersey: Prentice Hall.

Stewart, R. (1991). *Managing Today and Tomorrow*, London: MacMillan, especially Chapters 3, 4, 9, 10.

Smith, V. (1990). *Managing in the Corporate Interest*, University of California Press.

Issac-Henry, K. and Painter, C. (1991). *'The Management Challenge in Local Government - Emerging Themes and Trend's*, Local Government Studies, May/June.

Assistance from Richard Scase and Sarah Vickerstaff in compiling this case study is gratefully acknowledged.

Part 4
Organisational Processes

Case 14

JOB SATISFACTION AT OMEGA TECHNICAL SERVICES

Derek Adam-Smith and Alex Littlewood

A common approach to the assessment of levels of job satisfaction is through a survey of existing employee attitudes and opinions. The increased levels of absenteeism and labour turnover at Omega may be indicative of a low level of job satisfaction amongst employees. The case provides opportunities to examine methodologies used to determine employee attitudes and a discussion of the survey's implications. It also can be used as a basis for the wider analysis of attitudes and job satisfaction, their measurement, causal factors and potential strategies for improvement.

Question 1

Content of the attitude survey

The examination might begin with an analysis of the merits of the anonymous, essentially quantitative, questionnaire approach employed versus a more qualitative interview method. The benefits of the former approach as identified by the Personnel Manager in the text of the case need to be balanced with the richer information likely to be gained from an interview format which would have allowed particular points to be probed in more depth and for the strength of feelings to be assessed. The format of the questionnaire goes some way to overcoming these problems by including a set of open-ended questions to complement the quantitative information deduced from the closed questions. How far the actual wording of the open questions used and the information obtained from them overcome these limitations can be usefully discussed.

The Personnel Manager's concern with confidentiality reflects an organisational culture which apparently precluded the use of the interview method. In itself, this says much about the culture of the organisation and its possible implications for employee satisfaction.

Particular points that might be drawn out include:

- the use of a 'true/false' response to the questions can be compared with other approaches, for example, the Likert scale [discussed in McCormick and Ilgen (1987)] where a range of responses from strongly disagree through to strongly agree are offered.

- the beneficial use of questions to establish whether a particular factor is significant for an employee with a corresponding question to assess the level of satisfaction on that factor. Examples can be seen in Section (i) Nos. 53 and 60, 56 and 64; Section (ii) Nos. 3 and 61, 9 and 65; Section (iii) 16 and 30.

- the lack of any breakdown of job satisfaction scores, absenteeism or labour turnover rates on a regional basis which prevents, for example, any assessment of regional variation. Some judgement would need to be made as to how far the results of the survey can be used as a basis for making changes in the organisation. This should take account of the 'self-serving bias' where employees tend to blame factors outside their control for failure while taking credit themselves for things that are going well.

Question 2

Conclusions and recommendations

Robbins (1993) claims that global measures of job satisfaction such as the responses obtained to the first question are a more valid predictor of job satisfaction than summations of various job factors (as obtained by the bulk of the survey). A 50% level of satisfaction can be considered low when compared to other surveys (MORI, 1989).
Key conclusions which may be drawn from the data include:

- While general job satisfaction is low, there is clear evidence that employees find their jobs worthwhile, enjoying lack of boredom, variety, challenge and a sense of achievement. However, these benefits are being negated by extrinsic factors.

- performance is impeded by poor communications. Employees report insufficient involvement in decision making, little control over work matters and have little knowledge of activities at other regions.

- Clear evidence emerges of a perceived lack of fairness, care, support and feedback from management.

- Employees do not identify with the company and its objectives. With the results under communications this implies a weak corporate culture.

- Omega is seen as a short term employer; a high percentage reporting an active involvement in job search. Over half of respondents state they would leave for a 10% pay increase.

Attitude surveys tend to raise employees' expectations and a failure to act upon the results can be counterproductive since it may reinforce a view that management are not interested in employees' opinions.
The action plan developed will be a function of the conclusions drawn from the survey but it is likely that it will need to consider following matters:

Mission Statement

A vision of the company's future direction can provide guidance to both the organisation and employees of the behaviours which may contribute to its fulfilment.

Communications
Quantitative and qualitative improvements are needed to both horizontal and vertical

communication and the appropriateness of the methods available, e.g. employee reports, house journals, briefing sessions should be considered.

Management Style

The apparent high concentration on task achievement by managers may need to be complemented by recognition of the 'softer' motivational aspects of the management role.

Reward System

While constraints on pay may exist, a reward system that encourages experimentation and so develops learning in the workplace may be appropriate.

Performance Reviews

Whether or not linked to pay, regular reviews will encourage feedback to employees on their performance.

Participation

Greater involvement in decision making and the building of teamwork may exploit the entrepreneurial ideas existing within the company.

Recruitment

The selection process should seek to identify potential employees with a value system that is compatible with that of the organisation.

Training

Most of these recommendations will require training to ensure successful implementation and a training needs analysis will consequently need to be undertaken.

Trade Union Involvement

Whether, and at what stage, MSF should be involved in these changes should also be considered.

Further reading

Material on job satisfaction is voluminous, albeit of variable quality. The references in

Chapter 5 of Mullins (1993) provides a useful starting point.

MORI (1989). *Blueprint for Success: A Report on Involving Employees in Britain*, Industrial Society.

Case 15

QUALITY IMPROVEMENT IN PALL EUROPE

Roger Page and Alan Peacock

How the case can be used

This case study can be used to promote a number of activities that illustrate general aspects of human resource management as well as specific issues relating to total quality management, organisational culture, management style and the match between individual and organisational goals. The question set out in the activity brief can be used as a basis for role-play activities, to promote group discussion, or as written assignments.

The case can serve a number of learning objectives:

- To promote understanding of aspects of culture, management style and factors affecting the motivation and morale of employees.

- To demonstrate greater awareness of policies, procedures and practices that focus on a participative approach towards quality improvement.

- To consider and evaluate the costs and benefits to organisations and their employees of these policies, procedures and practices.

- To provide an opportunity of considering how the process of quality improvement can be applied to any work situation.

- To improve knowledge, skills and competence in problem-solving and communication in both formal and informal settings.

How the case relates to theory

The case relates to a number of issues relating to improving organisational performance and organisational processes. In particular, organisational culture, climate, and effectiveness, employee commitment, job satisfaction and work performance, management of change and the nature of management control. The situation described in the case can be used to explore the match between management style and the culture of an international organisation. The case will link well with organisational behaviour theory relating to individual aspects of motivation, attitude formation and the nature of products and services of an industrial organisation coping with the world recession.

Guidance for answers

Question 1

This question can be used to promote a written report from each student, or could be used as a vehicle for small group preparation and discussion and role play. Two groups could be formed and asked to view the culture and management style prevailing in the organisation from the position of employees or managers. Representatives of each group could be asked to prepare and present a critique of the process of quality improvement adopted by Pall and how it affects their working lives. Academic frameworks comparing strategies of management control e.g. Childs four strategies [see Mullins (1993), Fig 17.4 page 553] and link with the need to consider factors affecting human behaviour using theories of motivation, attitude formation and change. Comparisons could be made between management style and control systems that would be appropriate in organisations that adopt unitary or pluralistic frameworks. The influence of key managers in the case and how their personality has affected the implementation of the process could be used to illustrate behavioural and organisational issues relating to individual differences.

Question 2

This question is particularly appropriate for use as an activity promoting small group discussion comparing and contrasting the needs of the organisation with the needs of employees. The notion of total quality management and the claim that quality of work life can be improved by involving all employees in problem solving activities that consider issues affecting their working lives can be debated and related to conventional theories of motivation and attitude change. Examples drawn from the case could be used to compare reward systems and how they relate to possible reasons for employee or management resistance to the process of quality improvement. Financial rewards for the suggestion scheme can be compared and contrasted with the absence of financial rewards for successful quality work groups. The issue of continued quality improvements can be related to the long term and short term problems facing management who wish to maintain or increase improvements when the law of diminishing returns may affect the motivation and commitment of staff. Discussions could be encouraged that provide links with culture and management style addressed in **Question 1** and could affect the issues outlined in **Question 3** relating to the price of non conformance.

Question 3

This question provides an opportunity to replicate the activity of quality work groups and to consider the process of quality improvement by using an activity that will allow learning to be transferred by students to any work situation. The practical problems of generating workable ideas and interacting as an effective group will provide a further dimension for discussion. Evaluation of the price of non conformance (PONC) is a challenging task but has proved to be one of the essential requirements of the programme if appropriate relationships between satisfaction levels and reward expectation are to be maintained. Time saved is one method of evaluating benefit. A simple and obvious example in Pall was the use of Fax machines that seemed always to be receiving incoming messages when staff wished to send messages out. The simple solution provided was to use one Fax number for outgoing messages and a different one for incoming messages. The PONC was evaluated by an assessment of waiting time valued at £10 per hour less the additional Fax costs, a clear financial benefit has accrued and the remedy has removed a source of dissatisfaction amongst staff.

What happened

All employees at Pall Europe are committed to total quality management as described in the case. The structure is working well and staff are motivated towards continued improvement, some concerns are being expressed that in future savings will be more difficult to demonstrate and motivation difficult to maintain, however the target of '*zero defects*' is seen as the ultimate reward for effort. The culture and management style at Pall has been reinforced by the process and profitability increased. The largest savings in terms of PONC have been on production processes however the value to the organisation of improved commitment motivation and morale is perhaps the main benefit of the process.

Further reading

Potter, C. C. (1989). 'What is culture and how can it be useful for organisational change agents?', *Leadership and Organisational Development Journal*, Vol 10, No.3, pp 17—24.

Robson, M. (1988). *Quality Circles: a Practical Guide*, Second Edition, Gower.

Case 16

NEIGHBOURHOOD TEXTILES LTD

Motivation and Performance in a 'Top-Down' Co-operative Development Project

David Young and Tony Emerson

Using the case study

The Neighbourhood Textiles case study can be used as the basis for the discussion of theoretical and practical issues around local economic development, co-operative economic development and co-operative management. Since the project was a failure, however, it should be used with care, since many of the lessons to be drawn are illustrated in the negative. The case does not typify the co-operative experience.

Notes on Activity Brief Questions

Question 1

The commercial failure of Neighbourhood Textiles cannot credibly be explained as a simple, direct, or 'inevitable' consequence of its co-operative structure. Examples of commercial success and failure are as easy to find among co-operatives as they are among conventional businesses. Indeed, it is sometimes asserted that co-operatives have significantly higher survival rates than conventional businesses. However, the measurement and evaluation of commercial survival is methodologically problematic. For a discussion, see e.g. Cornforth et al (1988). The safest conclusion is that co-operatives survive at least as well as other types of firm.

Neighbourhood Textiles could have achieved commercial success under any system of management that enabled the firm to satisfy the key factors identified in the original feasibility study. The failure, then, was a failure to exploit real opportunities. The major trade customer who considered a buy-out of Neighbourhood Textiles evidently shared this assessment of opportunity.

The failure of Neighbourhood Textiles is best explained in terms of the operation of those factors which served to insulate the firm — fatally — from its opportunities. What is remarkable is that just about every factor in the environment in which Neighbourhood Textiles was developed and sought to survive can be seen to have contributed to its undermining. This includes internal factors, which can be traced to prior external factors. Under these circumstances, the degree of change necessary for the project to have succeeded would have been considerable. Numerous different 'success histories' can be imagined, but none would much — or usefully — resemble the actual environment and sequence of events.

Question 2

For a discussion of development models, see e.g. Paton and Emerson (1988), from which it is clear that the pure types of such models are seldom found in practice. Nevertheless, in general terms, the commitment and motivation of worker/members is not usually problematic in 'bottom-up' co-operative development projects, whereas in 'top-down' projects it often is. Neighbourhood Textiles is a rare example of a pure 'top-down' project, and was therefore particularly vulnerable to such problems.

The 'top-down' co-operative development model suffers from an inherent contradiction. Co-operation is an act of will, which can be fostered, but not enforced. The nearest enforceable approximation is contractual compliance, which is not enough. The co-operator must have a sufficient stake in the situation for his or her active co-operation to be meaningful. He or she must also be aware of the opportunity to co-operate, and of the means of co-operation. These principles apply to all types of organisation — officially 'co-operative' or otherwise.

In principle, the contradiction can eventually be resolved by the 'top' handing over control to a workforce whose development as true co-operators has been successfully fostered. This was an original intention of the Neighbourhood Textiles project. It is debatable that it could conceivably have been achieved in practice, not just because the voluntary surrender of power is uncommon, but because the 'top-down' development of the project ensured that major external stakeholders (Southminster, the Steering Committee) would necessarily remain in key roles for the foreseeable future.

In addition to these structural difficulties, however, further difficulties were caused by the near-total failure to train and develop the workforce as co-operators, despite original intent. This helped to ensure the failure of Management Committee meetings to manage, fostering the diversion of workers' attention from key issues, restricting the opportunity to co-operate, and the purpose of co-operation. The management structure, a bizarre mixture of the collective and the hierarchical, also militated against co-operation. It suggests a fundamental ambivalence on the part of the project's initiators — torn between a romantic fantasy of co-operation as a 'politically-correct' posture and an underlying mistrust of the workforce, tied to a basic reluctance to surrender power within the project, perhaps?

'Top-down' development occurs because developers wish to retain control over their stake in the project developed. It is thus likely to occur where e.g. substantial capital investment is required. The lesson is old and familiar within the co-operative movement — powerful external interests are not compatible with co-operative management (see for example, the history of the Rochdale Equitable Pioneers' Society, 1844—1862). Since the involvement of these interests was an essential ingredient in Neighbourhood Textiles' development, it is difficult to see how anything other than a 'top-down' model could have been used in practice.

73

Question 3

It is reasonable to expect a high level of self-motivation among co-operative worker/managers, for reasons discussed above. In the case of Neighbourhood Textiles, co-operation was originally a potential. This potential was partly realised in the induction training of Intake 1, but it was also squandered in part, because the training and development programme was not followed up as planned. Note, nevertheless, its success in establishing Intake 1 as an 'inner core' of co-operators. This points to what might have been achieved.

The induction of Intake 2 was a shambles, with no significant training, either in trade skills or in co-operative working. Here the opportunity to foster co-operation was again squandered. Thereafter, with means, opportunity and purpose denied, co-operative management was unlikely to develop.

Given the restrictions imposed upon the workforce, it is reasonable to question whether Neighbourhood Textiles was, in fact, a co-operative in any meaningful sense of the term. These restrictions were imposed by managers whose activities were visibly not effectively challenged by the Steering Committee. This failure surely undermined morale still further. Co-operative self-motivation had little chance to develop within the workforce, and every reason to degenerate into the alienation eventually identified by Acme Management Consultants.

A key argument to be considered here is that co-operative organisations provide a wider range of opportunity for performance outcomes than do hierarchical organisations. Hierarchy has the homeostatic virtues of safety and containment. Co-operation can exceed these bounds, but only because it may also fall below them.

Question 4

Given the results achieved by the partial training and development of Intake 1, it is reasonable to conclude that Neighbourhood Textiles might have performed differently had a thorough and competent training and development programme been provided, and formed the basis of an effective human resource development strategy within the organisation. No doubt Neighbourhood Textiles would have been far more successful than it was if every human resource factor had been optimised, but the fantasy overlooks the links between the non-human factors and the human factors in this case:

- The 'top-down' model was an inevitable ingredient in the development of such a project — its impact on human factors is discussed above.

- Southminster's objectives were always political, and it is likely that the Production Manager's appointment was politically-influenced. The insistence, against the evidence and original policy, that the *local* population held the necessary skills, can also be read as a politically-induced myopia.

- The Employment Department's failure to determine its EWS eligibility criteria, exacerbated by government spending cuts, was the cause of considerable avoidable delay and disruption, which upset the timing of the project, creating the need for a riskier launch plan - supplying a rationale for 'no-nonsense' management, the Production Manager's development of his personal power base, including the scrapping of the original human resources plan.

In these and other cases it is evident that human resource factors are closely linked to non-human factors. This is a self-evident corollary of the argument that an effective human resources strategy is vital to all aspects of an organisation's well-being. This suggests that human resource factors are a distinctive element within the organisational system, but only as an integral part of that system, and that their role and influence on organisational well-being cannot meaningfully be separated from non-human factors, in the case of Neighbourhood Textiles, or any other organisation.

Question 5

Numerous points of intervention by Production Workers or Steering Committee members can be imagined. The point is that the development of Neighbourhood Textiles, in structure and process, was resistant to democratic participation, and hence to intervention. It follows that any attempt at such intervention would probably have been diverted or neutralised.

It is argued here that the Steering Committee colluded to some extent in accepting the Production Manager's version of events, because of a fundamental ambivalence over the nature and purpose of the project — readers must judge for themselves. Workers, however, were denied the luxury of collusion, being denied access by management to effective democratic participation, to training and development opportunities, and to the information necessary to manage. They were instead diverted into such pseudo-debates as the conflict over childcare payments — another case of 'divide and rule'. This is the antithesis of co-operative working.

Further reading

Thornley, J. (1982). *Workers' Co-operatives — Jobs & Dreams*, Heinemann.

Oakeshott, R. (1978). *The Case For Workers' Co-ops*, Routledge and Kegan Paul.

Case 17

BROWNLOAF MACTAGGART — CONTROL AND POWER IN A MANAGEMENT CONSULTANCY

Gary Akehurst

How the case can be used

This case has different levels of complexity within it, and can be considered in a number of ways. At the heart of the case there are three main aspects:

- the organisational context, including corporate culture;
- the nature of power; and
- the nature of managerial control.

The case can also be used to consider quality assurance and the organisational structure required to deliver high quality consultancy services. In addition, issues such as the following can be explored:

- organisations as political systems (unitary, pluralist and radical) and the nature of conflict;
- organisational culture pre and post merger;
- organisations as coalitions of self-motivated and inner-directed individuals;
- leadership and management style;
- the motivation of highly educated and self-centred professionals; and
- the management of change in traditional professional firms.

Clearly this list is indicative rather than exhaustive and the tutor should carefully consider at the outset what are the main aspects to be examined, otherwise the case could be unwieldy; in particular, the tutor must ensure that students look beyond the apparent 'corporate jungle' of this case, with its elements of cynical, ruthless and selfish behaviour, the seize power and 'kick ass' culture and competitive environment.

How the case relates to theory

Watkins International and its constituent divisions needs to create and sustain order among its highly educated and highly paid employees, each of whom have diverse personal interests that can be a source of potential conflict. This conflict is always present, at personal and interpersonal level, between formal and informal groups, divisions and subsidiary organisations.

Watkins International is an organisation of semi-autonomous parts, each of which attempts to secure a measure of independence, while working within an organisational structure

76

established and maintained by the small elite of partners, who manage the affairs of the international firm, and make all the important strategic decisions. As this is a partnership, there are no shareholders or other stakeholders in the sense of an incorporated organisation.

Watkins displays strong autocratic tendencies, where ultimate power (that is, above divisional partner level) resides in a small group of executive partners. In no sense is Watkins a democratic organisation but it does tend towards bureaucracy — using Morgan's definition of 'rule is exercised through use of the written word, which provides the basis for a rational-legal type of authority, or 'rule of law" (1986, p. 145). Within a management consultancy however, we would have expected a 'technocracy', defined by Morgan as 'rule exercised through use of knowledge, expert power, and the ability to solve relevant problems' (1986, p. 145).

The case allows for an examination of power and how power bases may have changed as Brownloaf MacTaggart (BM) changed from a separate company to a small division of a much larger organisation. There is an opportunity to explore, among other things, the bases of power (of resources, dependency, etc.); the various power strategies open to BM partners, especially of reward, coercion, of legitimacy and resources controls; expert power by possession of specialist engineering knowledge, skills and information; networking or connection power and boundary management.

The issues of management control are complex but tutors may wish to explore issues such as the desirability of control in a management consultancy, the problems of control particularly through rules, quality assurance, rewards and punishments.

Guidance on answers to the questions set

Question 1

Identify the different ways in which managerial control and power are being exercised in both Watkins International as a whole and the BM Division in particular.

This question is relatively straight forward and serves as an introduction to the case by focusing on the key concepts of control and power. Management control must first be defined in the *positive* sense in that all people who have dealings with the organisation need to know what they have to do and when — this gives a desirable certainty, order and predictability. Control can also mean exploitation, coercion and manipulation. There are therefore, both desirable and undesirable aspects of control.

Huczynski and Buchanan define management control as 'the process through which plans are implemented and objectives are achieved by setting standards, measuring performance, comparing actual performance with standards, deciding necessary corrective action and feedback' (1991, p. 580).

Watkins partners can exercise control in many ways, through for example recruiting, promoting and dismissing employees; other controls include rewards, punishment, rules and policies, access to resources, staff appraisal and training.

According to Kakabadse, Ludlow and Vinnicombe, "power is essentially a firm base from which to act" (1988, p. 213). Various sources of power exist in Watkins International, and different strategies exist for using, developing and abusing that power.

Question 2

Having identified the different aspects of managerial control, examine how appropriate these are in managing the different types of employees in Watkins International.

Employees need to know what is expected of them. Control is one means of securing efficiency of resource use, creating a style and certain conditions to enable employees to work effectively. Watkins, and BM in particular, is really a relatively loose network of people with divergent interests, and each has a complex set of values, desires, expectations and goals. Coercion is likely to meet resistance, whether overt or covert. A sophisticated approach is therefore needed, which ensures timely and relevant feedback. Remember however, that Watkins does not only employ highly motivated and highly paid consultants; it also employs large numbers of support staff (secretarial, accounts, marketing, personnel, security, etc.) who can, at times, feel resentful of the high salaries of consultants.

Question 3

Explore the nature of the apparent dichotomy and tensions created, in allowing highly qualified, creative and essentially autonomous consultants room to reach creative solutions to client problems (often under considerable time pressures within an uncertain environment) and the employing organisation's need for order, stability and reliability.

Many consultants (particularly in BM) are essentially mavericks — independent in spirit and with only a relatively loose affiliation to their employing organisation. Their performance needs monitoring and, if necessary, corrective actions taken, otherwise there is an ever-present prospect of anarchy.

Consultants often feel that they cannot influence the outcomes of partner decision-making processes, and in large measure this is true. Insidious control, coercion, manipulation and domination are more than likely to lead to resistance, outright or (more likely) dumb hostility, and a significant drop in performance (however this is measured). Watkins relies to a large extent on company culture enforcing conformity, with a formal and informal staff appraisal system that weeds out undesirable or de-motivated staff. Client satisfaction within what can be very tight deadlines, requires however, strict control procedures that highlight at any stage of an assignment any potential problems. Watkins is scared of potentially damaging publicity, litigation, discontent or dissatisfaction from clients, who have, after all, usually paid considerable fees for the consultancy service.

Question 4

Considering the Watkins International approach to quality assurance, which appears to be primarily bureaucratic and perhaps at variance with the image management consultants would wish to present to clients, is this likely to affect the way consultants consider and make recommendations for the implementation of total quality management systems in client organisations?

Watkins introduced its quality management system in 1992 with the express intention of achieving the primary objective of providing high quality services to clients. The quality assurance system is designed to define and control management responsibility for quality (including review and internal quality audits), contacts with clients, control of assignments and resolution of any problems arising. On paper the system looks impressively comprehensive; in practice the system constrains rather than illuminates.

There is no reason why consultant frustration with the Watkins quality assurance system should unduly affect recommendations to clients or the implementation of quality systems in client organisations — if anything, consultants may be able, in the light of their own organisation's mechanistic response to quality issues, to devise somewhat better quality assurance procedures and systems.

What happened in practice

The situation in Watkins and the Brownloaf MacTaggart division continues much as described in the case. Business continues to be relatively slow and further cost cutting exercises have taken place (principally by reducing the number of employees). One or two consultants have succeeded in leaving BM for new jobs but generally life continues much as before.

Should this situation continue for much longer there is the possibility of a management buy-out in the BM division lead by Heinrich Grubber. Currently the BM division is awash with buy-out rumours. In all probability, over the next two years staff turnover (whether voluntary or involuntary) will reach 30 per cent per year, as the economy picks up. The BM partners are unlikely to seriously analyse and resolve their management problems but this will not stop them offering advice and solutions to the management problems of clients. This is a classic case of 'physician heal thy self'.

Further reading

The Recommended Reading is reasonably comprehensive but tutors may wish to explore inter-related issues, such as:

- the organisation as a political system (see Morgan, 1986, pp. 185 — 198);
- the restriction and liberation of individual development (see Braverman, H, 1974, *'Labour and Monopoly Capital: The Degradation of Work in the Twentieth Century'*, New York: Monthly Review Press);
- bureaucracy and roles (see Huczynski and Buchanan, 1991, Ch 16, pp. 398—428);
- managing 'know how' professionals such as consultants (see Sveiby and Lloyd, 1987, pp. 98—124).

Part 5
The Personnel Function

Case 18

DEALING WITH HIV/AIDS IN THE WORKPLACE

David Goss

The questions are intended to encourage readers to explore both the practical issues associated with HIV/AIDS policy and the behavioural and social processes which underpin any response. Given the debate which continues to surround HIV/AIDS it is likely that tutors will need to be prepared to confront issues relating to sexuality, illness, death and prejudice, issues that can often give rise to emotional and emotive responses.

Thus, in dealing with this case, it is essential that tutors not only exercise sensitivity but also gain a clear understanding of the medical facts relating to HIV and AIDS. Up-to-date information can normally be obtained from the health education department of the local council/health authority or from voluntary sector groups concerned with HIV/AIDS (e.g., National AIDS Trust, 6th Floor, Eileen House, 80 Newington Causeway, London, SE1 6EF, tel 071 972 2845; Terrence Higgins Trust, 52—4 Grays Inn Rd, London, WC1X 8JU, tel 071— 831 0330).

Question 1

In drafting a policy, the usual issue to address is the balance that can be achieved between protecting the interests of the employee/potential employee with HIV/AIDS on the one hand, and those of the organization on the other. Our research suggests that policies can vary between these two extremes: Humanistic (geared to protecting the individual) and Defensive (giving priority to organizational needs). Current thinking suggests that Humanistic policy represents 'best practice' and the 'Companies Act!' guidelines point towards such a response. An example of such a policy is shown below (Employment Department's booklet *AIDS and the Workplace*):

- The organization is committed to equality of opportunity in its employment. It is also committed to protecting and promoting the health of its employees.
- There will be no discrimination in recruitment against applicants internally or externally on the grounds that the applicant is HIV antibody positive or has AIDS.
- Applicants who are deemed to be fit at the time of interview will not be refused an offer to work because they have AIDS or are HIV antibody positive.
- If it becomes known that an employee has AIDS, the organization will ensure that resources are available to provide adequate support and will make any reasonable arrangements to enable work to be continued, on the grounds that to continue working may enable that person to maintain confidence and social contact and therefore fight AIDS with more dignity.
- Staff will not be dismissed because they have AIDS or redeployed to alternative employment unless they request it or medical advice states this is in the interest of the employee.
- Consideration will be given to requests for special leave by those who have

responsibility for caring for people with AIDS related diseases.

- No employee or applicant will ever be required to take the HIV antibody test.
- There should be no victimisation of an employee who is HIV antibody positive by others. Should victimisation occur, the medical facts about AIDS will be made available to the offending employee and she/he may also be given the opportunity to receive counselling about AIDS in the workplace.
- Employees who are HIV antibody positive or have AIDS are not required to inform the organization.
- However, if it became known that an employee has HIV infection/AIDS, confidentiality will be maintained. Deliberate breaches of this confidentiality by any other employee may constitute a disciplinary offence.

The distinction between Defensive and Humanistic policy has been discussed (with examples) in Adam-Smith et al (1992) and Goss et al (1993). See Further reading for details.

Question 2

In addition to the policy document itself, consideration should be given to the ways in which it can be put into practice and how this will effect existing personnel policy. For example, will there need to be a strong equal opportunities commitment both towards disability and sexual orientation? Will there need to be a programme of education, information and training: what form should this take and who will receive it? How can the policy be introduced without heightening needless fears about HIV/AIDS or 'flagging it up' as an abnormal or extreme problem? Practical responses to these issues are most fully addressed in texts focusing on equal opportunities. See Cockburn (1991) and Coussey and Jackson (1991).

Question 3

In terms of organisational behaviour the responses of employees will often be conditioned by factors associated with individual perceptions of 'normal' or 'acceptable' behaviour based on stereotyping (in the case of AIDS relating to homosexuality and drug abuse), frequently of a negative or stigmatising type. Perceptions of risk may also play a part in exaggerating the threat that HIV/AIDS poses in the workplace. One particular model, 'AIDS, nursing and occupational risk: an ethical analysis' by J. Sim, identifies three factors associated with any given hazard — 'magnitude', 'probability', and 'acceptability' — which together contribute to shaping individual responses to a hazard.

In relation to HIV/AIDS it seems that the factors of magnitude and probability are, in theory, amenable to relatively objective categorisation. The third factor — acceptability — relates not to objective or verifiable fact, but to questions of moral choice and subjective judgement. This is especially relevant in the case of AIDS because it is a disease which is defined not merely through medical concepts, but also through numerous 'layers' of morality, in particular the notion of homosexuality which has been characterised in much of the popular media as 'dangerous' and perverse. This latter component seems particularly important in determining

84

how much 'trust' individuals put in 'the facts', see Adam-Smith and Goss (1993). This is likely to be reinforced by work group cohesion and potential conflict between 'insiders' and 'outsiders'. In these respects the issue of HIV/AIDS is closely bound up with organisational power and control (i.e., managerial control to protect the organization's commercial/professional reputation, and the dominance of heterosexism in most organizations. For a theoretical discussion of the latter issue see Goffman (1963), Hearn et al (1989) and Hearn et al (1987)).

This sort of discussion gives rise to a number of ethical issues. For example, should organizations test potential or present employees for the HIV virus; should people who are HIV-positive or have AIDS have specific protection in employment law, see IDS (1993) and Wilson (1993); should there be closer surveillance of the health and personal habits of employees managers might suspect of being at risk of contracting HIV?

Further reading

Adam-Smith, D. and Goss, D. (1993). 'HIV/AIDS and the hospitality industry: some implications of perceived risk', *Employee Relations*, Special Edition, 15,2

Adam-Smith, D., Goss, D., Sinclair, A., Rees, G., Meudell, K. (1992). 'AIDS and employment: diagnosis and prognosis', *Employee Relations,* 18, 3, pp. 29—40.

Cockburn, C. (1991). *In the Way of Women*, London: Macmillan

Coussey, M and Jackson, H. (1991). *Making Equal Opportunities Work*, London: Pitman.

Goffman, E. (1963). *Stigma*, London: Penguin.

Goss, D., Adam-Smith, D., Sinclair, A., Rees, G. (1993). 'AIDS policies as data: possibilities and precautions', *Sociology*, 27,2.

Hearn, J., Sheppard, D., Tancred-Sheriff, P. and Burrell, G. (Eds), (1989). *The Sexuality of Organization*, London: Sage.

Hearn, J. and Parkin, W. (1987). *Sex at Work: the Power and Paradox of Organization Sexuality*, Brighton: Wheatsheaf.

IDS (1993). *AIDS returns to the Agenda*, IDS Study 528.

Keay, D. and Leach, M. (1993). 'Positive thinking about HIV', *Human Resources*, Spring, pp. 36—40.

Sim, J. (1992). 'AIDS, nursing and occupational risk: an ethical analysis' *Journal of Advanced Nursing*, 17, pp. 569—575.

Wilson, P. (1993). *HIV and AIDS in the Workplace*, London: National AIDS Trust.

Case 19

CHANGING SHIFTWORKING ARRANGEMENTS IN AN NHS HOSPITAL TRUST

David Farnham

How the case can be used

This case study illustrates some of the problems of managing change. It illustrates the importance of involving those who are affected by change in organizations and the importance of establishing good working relations between managers and well organized, and cohesive, professional staff. It also illustrates the importance of reaching a negotiated compromise where there are conflicts between management and organized groups of workers, covered by negotiating procedures.

Answers to questions

Question 1

The unitary and pluralist frames of reference and their application to employee relations are well known. Students who are unfamiliar with the terms, or who need to revise the concepts, can be referred to Farnham and Pimlott (1990, Chapter 1). Students wanting a more detailed analysis can refer to Fox's work, such as *Man Mismanagement* (1974), which explores the unitary and pluralist concepts more fully and also provides a critique of them.

Question 2

The relevance of social action theory to employee relations is also considered by Farnham and Pimlott (1990, Chapter 1) and by Jackson, *An Introduction to Industrial Relations* (1991). A detailed exploration of social action theory is provided by Silverman, *The Theory of Organizations* (1970).

Question 3

The *status quo* provision of the existing procedure to avoid disputes is to enable: (1) *negotiated change* to take place on variations to conditions of service and working practices; (2) prevent either side taking industrial action against the other, whilst matters of common concern are under discussion; and (3) legitimize any joint decisions taken by the parties within the negotiating machinery.

If management no longer wishes to be bound by the *status quo* clause, because it slows down the decision taking process, one way of doing this is to give written notice of its intention, under the terms of the agreement, to terminate the agreement. This might provoke the unions into taking some kind of industrial action and management must have contingency plans for dealing with this.

Question 4

The night staff's responses to the proposal to change their shiftworking arrangements were:

Standardization

This was a reasonable objective. It was unsatisfactory for shift times to be different on three different wards in the same unit but it had to be done in consultation with them.

Overlap

The night shift unanimously agreed that 17 minutes was insufficient time to hand over their duties to the next shift, especially where patients had been admitted over-night as emergencies and required surgery.

Equalization of shifts

This would result in night staff working eight nights on and six nights off or four nights on and three nights off. There would be difficulty in adjusting from day to night shifts or from nights to days. It could result in an increase in staff sickness, requiring staff to be replaced by expensive agency staff who are less effective than regular staff and have little or no experience in this area of nursing.

Social acceptability of shifts

This was not a major problem for staff but they wanted the dispute to be resolved before acknowledging this.

Minimizing payments for unsocial hours

This was seen by the night staff as a threat, since it was perceived that if the night shift was not reduced, and money saved, there would be a cut in staffing levels.

Question 5

The root issue was the behaviour of the Cardio-Thoracic Unit Manager and her insensitivity to the managing of change. The staff felt that she was using her management prerogative with little consideration of the outcome. They considered that she lacked insight into the real problems facing the night shift and that she was not working to the same goal as the nursing staff, i.e. patient care. The manager was also seen by the staff to anti-union and saw the union as being obstructive, difficult and intrusive on the right to manage. The whole issue could have been avoided by a more consultative and participative approach by the Cardio-Thoracic Manager with the nursing staff.

Question 6

The solutions suggested from students can be compared with the final outcome which was:

- All staff employed prior to the beginning of the current financial year (5 April) would remain on their current contracted hours, unless they changed their hours by going from full time to part time or the number of staff fell below five, at which point the position would be reviewed.

- The new shift times, subject to discussions with the day staff, would start with effect from 26 October. All staff who had started new contracts since 5 April would work the new shifts.

- All agency or excess hours would be worked to the new shifts.

- Staff appointed before 5 April would continue to work their old hours of 1945 — 0645.

Further reading

Fox, A. (1974). *Man Mismanagement*, London: Hutchinson.

Jackson, M. (1991). *An Introduction to Industrial Relations*, London: Routledge.

Silverman, D. (1970). *The Theory of Organisations*, London: Heinemann.

Case 20

EMPLOYEE CAPABILITY IN A MAGISTRATES COURT

Alan Peacock

How the case can be used

This case study can be used to promote a number of activities that heighten awareness of general aspects of human resource planning and development as well as specific issues relating to discipline at work in the difficult area of capability. All three questions can be used as a basis for role-play activities, to promote group discussion, or as written assignments. The case can serve a number of learning objectives:

- To promote understanding of legislation relating to unfair dismissal.

- To demonstrate greater awareness of policies, procedures and practices that match individual and organisational needs.

- To consider and evaluate the costs and benefits to organisations and their employees of these policies, procedures and practices.

- To provide an opportunity of considering the social responsibilities of managers who are required to deal with difficult human relations problems.

- To improve knowledge, skills and competence in problem-solving and communication in both formal and informal settings.

How the case relates to theory

The case deals with a number of human resource management issues relating to employee resourcing, employee development and employee relations. In particular, the evaluation of the Magistrates Courts' recruitment, selection, performance appraisal and personal development policies procedures and practices relate to employee resourcing and employee development whilst the legal and behavioural issues of disciplinary action relate to aspects of employee relations. The situation described in the case can be used to explore the match between organisational needs and the needs of managers and employees and will link well with organisational behaviour theory relating to individual aspects of motivation, attitude formation and the social responsibility of managers in organisations.

Guidance for answers

Question 1

This question can be used to promote a written report from each student or could be used as a vehicle for small group preparation and discussion. To avoid repetition each group could be asked to prepare and present a critique exploring different aspects of employment practice as illustrated by the situation described in the case — for example recruitment and selection — or by using different academic frameworks e.g. those from Schein's Career Dynamics (1978), or Mullins (1993) that focus on personal development, particularly those described in Part 7. A further activity could be introduced in which students are asked to argue a case for improvements to the personnel policies procedures and practices of the magistrates court based on the written report. The facilitator may wish to link the behavioural implications of good employment practice with economic benefits gained by the organisation through the effective use of human resources.

Question 2

This is particularly appropriate for simulating the operation of an industrial tribunal. A group of students can be asked to adopt roles and present a case before an industrial tribunal. In this event three students are given roles as the chairperson and the two 'lay officials' of the tribunal. They will hear the case and pass judgement. Other students will be asked to prepare the case for the applicant and provide role-players to act as the applicant, his representative(s) and witnesses. A third group will act in similar capacities on behalf of the respondent. The tutor can act as facilitator by providing each group with legal advice and access to legal information. Specific scripts can be written for each role if particular emphasis is required on any aspect of the case. Information and guidance on the procedural aspects of presenting cases before an industrial tribunal should be available to students. If time is available, closed-circuit television (CCTV) can be used as a feedback mechanism and used to evaluate skills and competencies associated with the role-play activities.

In presenting the case, students should demonstrate an awareness of the law relating to unfair dismissal and in particular the issues relating to capability. Reference texts such as Smith and Wood (1989) or Croner's or Harvey's employment guides (see Further reading) will provide a structured pattern for considering legal issues and provide summaries of appropriate case law in this area. The ACAS Code of Practice indicates the statutory procedural requirements. A summary of legal requirements, good employment practice and a checklist outlining how managers should handle a disciplinary matter relating to capability can be found in Peacock (1993).

Question 3

This question can be used for small group discussion, written assignment or unseen time constrained examination. (The case study material but not the question should be given to students in advance.) These activities provide an opportunity to explore the role and function of managers in organisations, corporate goals and values including business ethics and to relate these to the expectations of employees individual managers and employees. Dismissal from employment on grounds of ill health on the short and long term well being of the organisation is often affected by the personal feeling of managers and their concern for the well being of the unfortunate employee and family. Managers who are required to make such decisions must take proper account of the needs of the organisation and the needs of employees.

In the situation described, the role of the employee is crucial to the outcome. Mr French's medical condition will prevent him from discharging vital parts of his role as Magistrates Clerk. He suffers from short blank periods where he temporarily loses consciousness, this may mean that he does not hear all the evidence placed before the court by a defendant. His role is to advise the magistrates on matters of law and he may not be able to do this adequately if he misses vital evidence. It could be however that managers could fulfil their social responsibility to the court defendants and Mr French by offering him suitable alternative employment in a role that will not be affected by his medical condition.

References for the legal issues have been given for **Question 2**, the role of the effective managers and the balance between social responsibility and effective performance are considered by Mullins (1993), particularly Gatewood and Carrol (1991) focus on ethical performance, the work of Schein and Mullins referred to in **Question 1** can be used to consider possible alternative employment.

What happened

In reality Mr French was removed from his job as Magistrates Clerk and offered alternative employment as a Conveyancing Assistant with terms and conditions unaffected. He felt that this was not suitable alternative employment. The employer therefore dismissed him on grounds of capability. Mr French complained to an Industrial Tribunal that he had been unfairly dismissed but his complaint was not upheld. The organisation reviewed the policies procedures and practices relating to recruitment, selection, appraisal and personal development and found that the systems were in place but were not operating effectively. Initiatives were taken to ensure that practice followed the agreed policies and procedures.

Further reading

ACAS Code of Practice number 1 (1977). *Disciplinary Practice and Procedure in Employment*; together with the ACAS handbook on *Discipline at Work*, first published in 1987.

Blue Star Ship Management Ltd v Williams (1979). IRLR 16

Croner's Reference Book for Employers, New Malden: Croner Publications.

Employment Protection Consolidation Act 1987, s. 57.(4).

Gatewood, R. D. and Carroll, A. B. (1991). 'Assessment of ethical performance of organisational members: a conceptual framework'. *Academy of Management* , Review 16.

Harvey, R. J. *Harvey on Industrial Relations and Labour Law*, London: Butterworth.

Mullins, L. J. (1993). *Management and Organisational Behaviour*, London: Pitman.

Peacock, A. (1993). 'A managers guide to unfair dismissal' *Administrator*, May.

Case 21

MIDSHIRE ASSOCIATION FOR THE BLIND — THE STAFFING IMPLICATIONS OF RESTRUCTURING

Irene Watson

How to use the case study

This case study can be used to examine a range of issues to do with individuals, groups and organisations including:

- individual behaviour, change and stress;
- motivation, communication, influence and control;
- management roles and responsibilities;
- organisational goals and social responsibility;
- employment law, contractual issues.

Guidance on the answers to the Activity Brief

Question 1

In the policy and procedure devised by the MAB Personnel Officer, the strengths, weaknesses and omissions include:

- The introductory statement of intent towards job security and the objective of treating employees fairly and reasonably are strengths.

- The outline of measures for minimising or avoiding redundancies is quite well written. Some are mentioned and the way is left open for others; if too many are mentioned, the list may be taken to be complete whereas all suggestions should be considered.

- It is good to see the commitment to consultation at the earliest opportunity even though there are no recognised trade unions — case law has determined that individuals should be consulted.

- The criteria for selection for redundancy are weak. The first is too general and could be applied subjectively. The second, length of service (LIFO) is objective but may not be appropriate and may have equal opportunities implications. Multiple, clearly defined, objective criteria may be stated in a procedure or the clause left open with the comment that criteria will be selected, subject to consultation, to fit the circumstances of each situation as it arises. More objective criteria include performance, skills, qualifications, age, attendance and disciplinary record.

- It is not really necessary to give details of notice but it would be useful to explain what would happen to employees who wish to leave before they are given notice or before their notice expires, i.e. whether they forfeit their redundancy compensation.
- If there is need to retain employees until an agreed date (more common in closures than staff reductions), there could be mention of measures to encourage them to stay, e.g. terminal bonuses.

- It is a strength to spell out the circumstances surrounding offers of alternative employment since employers have a duty to try to identify such opportunities.

- It is advisable to separate statutory from any additional redundancy compensation so there can be no confusion at a later date about what employees have received.

- A major omission is mention of any non-financial measures to assist redundant employees. Some measures, e.g. time off to look for work or arrange training, are statutory but many employers offer other forms of help — counselling, job search training, advice about benefits and personal finances, information about self-employment, guidance on further education or training, early retirement advice, etc. It is a motivating factor if these measures are available to all redundant staff and not just to a selected few.

- Where redundancy is affecting only a proportion of employees or where there are selection criteria which could be applied subjectively, it would be appropriate to include an appeal procedure so that employees can challenge decisions they feel are unfair.

Question 2

The Chief Executive's action plan for implementing the reorganisation in MAB should take into consideration:

- an overall timescale and end date;
- the legal requirements for consultation;
- time for real consultation on the policy and procedure as well as the new organisation, consideration of comments and the response;
- training for managers in communication and counselling skills;
- group and individual meetings with employees;
- publication of and briefing on new personnel policies and procedures;
- meetings with voluntary workers;
- a system of continuing briefings;
- informing clients of implications of change;
- public relations press release.

The way proposals for radical change which may lead to redundancy are announced

95

influences the reaction of employees:

- Mass meetings ensure that all employees have the same knowledge at the same time but are impersonal, so the information given should be limited to general issues; detail is better imparted at small group briefings. Mass or group meetings help build group support and prevent rumour.

- Individual face-to-face meetings are essential for detail and where the issue is personal, i.e. the fact rather than the threat of redundancy, as it allows the individual to take in the knowledge and react to it in private.

- Individually in writing is appropriate as confirmation only.

In the longer term, the plan should include:

- timescales for appointments to the new positions;
- notice periods for those who are leaving;
- appeals against selection for redundancy;
- arrangements for non-financial measures to alleviate effects of redundancy.

Question 3

Employees' response to announcements of reorganisation, especially when presented as consultation leading to possible redundancy, is likely to include anxiety and questions about the future. The longer the uncertainty goes on, the worse the anxiety and stress gets. Information is the key to reducing anxiety; the period of uncertainty should be kept as short as possible consistent with real consultation.

Employees' reaction to the news of reorganisation and/or redundancies changes over time. The immediate response to news of redundancy includes:

- anger: allow the employee to 'burn out' without interruption;
- emotion and tears: stay with the employee until outburst is over;
- silence: encourage the employee to talk it out.

Managers should be aware that their authority is diminished amongst redundant employees; formal control is reduced and they have to rely on the employees' self esteem and goodwill. In the longer term, most employees will work exceptionally hard to tie up loose ends and leave everything tidy. This is essential to their self esteem and enables them to leave feeling that they have done everything they can. They are frequently concerned about clients or customers, especially in an organisation like MAB, and this concern should be anticipated and allayed through reassurance and information. If employees are denied this opportunity to 'close', this part of the 'grieving' process, it hinders their ability to recover, move on and find another job.

96

Many employers are afraid of industrial sabotage, that employees under notice will have a disruptive influence or are embarrassed at the thought of having the employees around. They demonstrate their distrust and embarrassment by refusing to permit employees to work out their notice, thus damaging their future prospects.

Question 4

Employees who keep their jobs whilst colleagues are redundant often feel confused — a mixture of relief and guilt — and the result can be a temporary loss of performance.

Measures to maintain motivation and morale amongst employees during the reorganisation should include:

- regular and full communications with all staff;
- being seen to be fair in selection for redundancy;
- generous compensation;
- programmes of retraining, career counselling, job search training, etc. for those who are redundant.

Afterwards, employees want to get back to 'normal' as quickly as possible and new directions could be reinforced through:

- communication, team briefing, etc.;
- training for new and future roles.

Question 5

A good employer will attempt to fill vacancies resulting from reorganisation from within the staff rather than by declaring employees redundant and, in any event, MAB's Security of Employment Policy and Procedure refers to trying to find alternative employment for redundant employees. The procedure used for selecting employees to fill vacancies must be and be seen to be effective and fair to all concerned but, these are both rather subjective terms which can be difficult to define.

To be both effective and fair in which ever method of selection is chosen, the procedure must be open and preferably subject to consultation with those who will use it.

Possible methods of making appointments include:

(a) All new positions being advertised and employees invited to apply; this may be effective in some ways but would be time consuming for both managers and applicants. It would be fair in that everyone would have an equal opportunity to apply but could raise questions about what constitutes a 'new' job from those who feel they are already performing that job.

(b)   A matching process where the duties and responsibilities of each new job are compared with those of the existing job and if there is, say, a 50% or greater match, the existing post-holder appointed; if there is less than a 50% match the position is advertised. This can be effective, in that it can get people into post quickly but can result in a poor match and no account is taken of the ability of the employees. It could be open to accusations of unfairness in the matching process.

(c)   Employees could be invited to complete some form of personal profile, detailing qualifications, experience, skills and preferences for new jobs, and the information used to make appointments in a similar way to (b) above. This would be effective in that it is based on employees preferences but no account is taken of ability. Again, it could be open to accusations of unfairness in the matching process.

(d)   Managers could make appointments from their personal knowledge of employees. This would only be effective and fair if based on an open performance appraisal system but not if on personal preferences.

Whichever method is used, there are certain factors which will help to ensure that the process is effective and fair:

- detailed job descriptions and candidate specifications for the new jobs and, in the case of (b) above, current job descriptions of the old jobs as well;

- in addition to the line manager, an independent manager or the Personnel Officer being involved in the matching or selection process;

- if, for any given post or posts, there is a surplus of suitable employees, the decision to be made by interview by managers trained in selection interviewing;

- feedback to all unsuccessful candidates to explain reasons for decisions;

- an appeal procedure involving people not party to the original selection decision.

Further reading

The IPM Library and Information Service can provide details of current books, research documents, surveys, case law and journal articles on this topic.

Case 22

COMPETENCE BASED RECRUITMENT AND SELECTION

Marjorie Corbridge and Stephen Pilbeam

This case outlines a competence based approach to recruitment and selection. The rationale for this approach is predicated on the following:

- Demographic projections and changes in the workforce profile, in particular a decreasing number of young people entering the workforce and increased economic activity amongst women and older workers, make it prudent to seek opportunities to recruit from a wide range of sources.
- Promoting equality of opportunity by challenging stereotyping in relation to age, gender and ethnic origin through recruiting and selecting fairly, consistently and on merit.
- Facilitating the entry into the organisation of people who can actually do the job because the focus of recruitment and selection is on specific job and organisational requirements.
- Extending the use of competence assessment into another area of Human Resource Management. Current applications include training and development and appraisal related pay based on the assessment of competence.
- Linking in with National Vocational Qualifications, which are competence based, and the work being done by the Management Charter Initiative and the Training and Development and Personnel Lead Bodies.

The case may also stimulate wider discussion in the areas of:

- Job analysis and its techniques
- Recruitment activity
- Selection methods
- Demographic change
- Labour markets
- Equality of opportunity
- The concept of competence and the competence debate

As indicated in the text it is not intended to 'sell the big idea', but sensitize students on the one hand to the importance, processes and outcomes of recruitment and selection and on the other to this concept of competence and its potential applications.

It may help to provide a practical illustration. For example in an administrative position which requires interaction with the public, the core competences may include:

- Getting on with other people

- Effective oral communication ability
- Effective written communication ability
- The ability to adapt to change
- Accurate interpretation and use of data
- The ability to prioritise tasks
- Effective decision making

This is a list of things that the individual has to be able to do in order to perform the job successfully. It becomes apparent that there is a degree of difficulty associated with assessing these competences through the use of traditional criteria such as academic qualifications or drawing inferences from previously held work or job positions. The focus of attention needs to be on establishing what will facilitate the recognition of good and poor levels of competence. This involves determining positive and negative behavioural indicators and deciding what evidence is required of the candidates.

Developing this theme, and addressing the assessment of the competence relating to effective oral communication, positive behavioural indicators may include:

- Clear and confident delivery
- The provision of concise answers to questions
- The ability to use questioning techniques to obtain relevant information

Conversely, negative or contra indicators may include:

- Talks excessively
- Lack of coherence in answering questions
- Lack of awareness of questioning techniques

Evidence could be collected through face-to-face contact with the candidate.

The examples in this case study are limited principally to a competency analysis of existing job descriptions, which may be supplemented by student knowledge and experience. However students may wish to develop more organisationally specific competency analysis methods and this approach can be explored in more detail in appropriate group discussion.

The selection of recruitment method to attract candidates serves a number of purposes:

- It communicates clearly the nature of the job and what the job holder will have to do.
- It offers a more realistic preview of the job and what will be expected.
- It is more likely to attract applicants from a wider range of sectors of the potential workforce by moving the emphasis away from traditional factors such as age and educational achievement.
- Conversely it may encourage unsuitable applicants to self select out at the recruitment stage by enabling them to make decisions about whether they want or are indeed suitable for the job.

Continuing with our example the application form may include questions along the following lines:

Oral communication ability

> 'As an administrative assistant you will need to be able to communicate effectively with members of the public, sometimes in testing circumstances. Please produce illustrations of when you have had to deal with difficult people or situations and how you have communicated effectively.'

This approach provides information on the agreed competences, which will help in the shortlisting or screening process, and continues to exploit the benefit of offering realistic job previews.

An example of tasks to be included in the recruitment and selection of an administrative assistant could be for the job holder to interpret numerical information or check the accuracy of data and again it may be possible to test these competences through the development of relatively simple tests.

Ultimately a battery of selection methods could be developed and incorporated into a competence based assessment centre. This is obviously beyond the scope of this case study, but the additional reading includes examples of organisations that are pursuing this approach.

Before we leave our selection methods it is relevant to identify that this focus on competence can be extended to the pursuit of personal and work references. An example of a question asked of a referee may be:

> 'Please indicate to what extent you believe this applicant (has the competence of) or (is able to make) effective decision making. What leads you to this view?'

Clearly some idea of task content and job context would be essential before it could be appropriate to expect reference respondents to answer this type of question.

The suggested activities are designed to enable the student to demonstrate an understanding of the difference between a competence approach and a traditional age, qualification and previous job approach. It will also be useful to make the link between training and development and competence and the complementary aspect of this approach. Organisations who are well down the road in the introduction of competence in training needs analysis will find this approach works well not just in external recruitment but in internal promotion and transfer. There are companies who have used it for the identification of suitable internal candidates who have found that transfers and promotions have taken place very successfully in what they describe as 'non-traditional' job flows.

Activities

Questions 1 and 2

These are very practical and focus on the student undertaking an activity, e.g. producing a job description and preparing an interview schedule. It is important not to be too prescriptive in looking for 'one right answer' but to ensure that the student has identified competence and that the behaviour that is being looked for is clear. There may be more difficulty in defining performance indicators but again these should be both quantitative and qualitative and both good and poor levels defined.

Question 3

The students should be encouraged to look critically at this approach and there are different ways of doing this.
Discussions on the costs of recruitment and selection and what contributes to costs e.g.
- Job analysis
- Advertising
- Administration
- Interviewing and testing
- Travel and accommodation
- Labour turnover
- Induction
- Initial training

This is not an exhaustive list but it is interesting to compare (or attempt to compare) costs between traditional and competence approach.

Question 4

Again this is an attempt to promote discussion on how to evaluate effective recruitment. There are examples in the additional reading on how this can be done and also what some of the difficulties may be.

Further reading

Connock, S. (1992). 'The Importance of 'Big Ideas' to Human Resource Managers', *Personnel Management*, June, pp. 24-27.

Cockerill, T. (1989). 'The Kind of Competence for Rapid Change', *Personnel Management*, September, pp. 52–6.

Glaze, T. (1989). 'Cadbury's Dictionary of Competence', *Personnel Management*, July, pp. 44–8.

Greatrex, J. (1989). 'Oiling the Wheels of Competence', *Personnel Management*, August, pp. 36-39.

Jacobs, R. (1989). 'Getting the Measure of Management Competence', *Personnel Management*, June, pp. 32-387.

Lewis, P. (1992). *Competences: The Mortar that Holds Together HRM Bricks?* IPM Tutors Conference, Manchester.

Woodruffe, C. (1991). 'Competent by Any Other Name', *Personnel Management*, September, pp. 30-33.

Part 5
Improving Organisational Performance

Case 23

HALFORDS - A TEN YEAR PROGRAMME OF ORGANISATIONAL RENEWAL: 1982—92

Tom McEwan

How the case can be used

The case, which has been updated, has been used successfully on MBA Management Development courses for several years. The main aims have been to explore the impact of organisational change, brought about by the recession and the contrasting cultures of three different owners within six years. The main task facing senior management during this turbulent decade was how to transform Halfords diverse range of high-street retail shops into a chain of modern, edge-of-town superstores. This entailed the introduction of new technology, 'downsizing' of manpower requirements, increased responsibilities for store managers and their deputies; and an ongoing programme of staff retraining and development. These changes were accompanied by a fluctuating financial performance which ranged from modest profits to disturbing losses for the company.

The chief benefit to students in analysing the case is that it anticipates many of the unavoidable structural changes which are currently being experienced by many British companies. It therefore provides an opportunity for 'action learning' by enabling students to analyse the various events and policies implemented by different senior managers at Halfords and compare these with the strategies adopted towards organisational change and development within their own organisations.

How the case relates to theory and the headings listed above

Most of the events described in the case may be analysed within the related frameworks of leadership [Mullins (1992), Chapter 8], organisational development [Mullins (1992), Chapter 20], management development and effectiveness [Mullins (1993), Chapter 21], and the implementation of strategic change [Johnson and Scholes (1993), Chapter 11].

Organisational theory, supported by field studies, indicates that successful change is only possible if senior management makes a sustained effort to improve the organisation's problem-solving and renewal processes. This means that a collaborative diagnosis of organization culture is essential. Special emphasis must also be placed on developing formal work teams alongside temporary teams, often with the aid of a qualified consultant, as a way of changing culture at the inter-group and the organisational levels. Identification of the nature and sources of conflict within organisations is also necessary. Particular attention must be focused on understanding any resistance to change to ensure that this is addressed in an even-handed and systematic manner. All of these issues are explored in the case.

Guidance on answers to the questions at the end of the case

Question 1

By the time that Ian S took over, the power of the 'Old Halfordians' had been considerably weakened and it is safe to assume that those who remained had decided to accept the new organisation culture. Ian S therefore had the immediate task of raising staff morale and improving employee commitment. He also had the added advantage of being regarded as the 'training champion' of Halfords. Students should identify examples of his efforts to raise morale by giving staff a sense of importance in their jobs, developing teamwork, indicating how much he and his fellow senior managers cared about staff welfare, and ensuring that economic rewards were fair and individualised. His aim should be improve staff commitment by developing a sense of belonging to the new Halfords organisation, as well as a sense of excitement based on pride, trust and personal accountability for results; and greater confidence in and respect for the authority, dedication and competence of the new management team.

Question 2

The principal stakeholders in the Halfords organisation have clearly altered with each change in ownership. Company directors and shareholders aside, the most important stakeholders were probably the successive Halfords chief executives whose different leadership styles had a profound impact on the organisational culture. The leadership styles varied from the paternalistic approach of Mr H, with its attendant inefficiencies, to the more autocratic, path-goal approach adopted by Roger P, followed by the greater emphasis on action-centred leadership adopted by Ian S [Mullins (1992), Chapter 8]. Students should be able to recognise the strengths and weaknesses of the first two of these three styles of leadership from the way that the first approach retarded necessary organisational renewal within Halfords, whereas the second approach achieved short-term financial goals but at the expense of damaging staff morale and commitment.

Question 3

Field studies in Britain and the USA reveal that staff development and training programmes, alongside research and development, are the first to suffer during a period of recession. However, the medium to long-term consequences are that untrained labour is unable to meet the technological demands of an economic upturn and employers have to pay a premium to attract essential skilled labour. Not for nothing does trade union membership increase as an economy moves out of, rather than into, or during a recession. In short, there are sound economic reasons why the Halfords senior management should continue with their strategy of introducing greater efficiency measures alongside ongoing staff training and development programmes to ensure that the company is best placed to exploit the competitive advantage it has over its smaller rivals once the UK economy emerges from the current recession.

What happened in practice, or likely outcomes of issues not yet resolved

Events are summarised in the case as they occurred and the main unresolved issue is trying to second-guess how the Boots Company plc will respond to the recent poor financial results recorded by its Halfords subsidiary. City editorial opinion, based on knowledge of the Boots Company plc previous strategic policy, suggests that the company tends to adopt a prudent, long term approach towards is diversification policy. Its main activities include pharmaceutical manufacturing and retailing and both of these divisions out-performed their market-sector during 1991—92, suggesting that the Halfords subsidiary is unlikely to be closed down or sold off to a fourth owner within less than ten years.

Further reading

Stacey, R. (1993). *Strategic Management and Organisational Dynamics,* London: Pitman. Chapters 4 to 11 examine traditional, emergent and extraordinary management strategies for coping with organisational change in an original, well-researched manner.

Hurst, D. K., Rush, J. C. and White, R. E. (1989). 'Top Management Teams and Organisational Renewal', *Strategic Management Journal,* Vol 10, pp. 89—105. Develops a creative management model which goes beyond conventional strategic management and identifies the behaviour needed for ongoing renewal of a business organisation.

Mezias, S. J., and Glynn, M. A. (1993). 'The Three Faces of Corporate Renewal: Institution, Revolution and Evolution', *Strategic Management Journal,* Vol 14, pp. 77—101. Examines corporate renewal from a structured approach by focussing on essential routines and rules and develops two further approaches which involve international efforts to encourage innovation either within or, more revolutionary, by moving away from the accepted organisational paradigm.

Stayer, R. (Nov-Dec 1990). 'How I learned to let my workers lead', *Harvard Business Review,* pp. 66—83.

Case 24

THE POSITION AND CONTRIBUTION OF SUPPORT SERVICES TO AN NHS TRUST

Jeff Watling and Tony Strike

How the case can be used

This case will be of particular interest to managers in public sector organisations, particularly the NHS. However, it is likely to be of interest to those working in large, private sector organisations and in service departments such as personnel, marketing and finance.

The case will lend itself to group working. For **Questions 1 and 2** the students can be divided into teams of 4—6 to prepare oral presentations in support of the pharmacy or personnel approaches to date, or the benefits of a centralist against a 'Clinical Directorate' or devolved approach.

Questions 3,4 and 5 provide the opportunity to turn the case around and encourage the student to look at services from the customer's point of view. These questions demand a more reflective response and therefore are best undertaken as individual activities.

How the case relates to theory

Before assessing the activities of the departments concerned it will be of value to examine the two service departments and the individuals within them in the context of the NHS and the Trust in which they are based. A number of models are available for this purpose. The headings listed under *Interrelated influences on behaviour in work organisations* [Mullins (1993), p. 15, Figure 1.12] or the Hersey & Blanchard or the Leavitt models [Mullins (1993), p. 74] are all appropriate for this purpose. Internal analysis, examining the services provided, financial performance, people and organisational issues, followed by SWOT analysis [Mullins (1993), p. 99—100] will help the group to focus on the key internal and external issues for each department.

Chapter 5, Organisation Structure and Systems, will assist in establishing appropriate structural relationships for service departments, as will Chapter 8, The Nature of Management, particularly the section on the Personnel Function. (p. 209).

The Purchaser/Provider split will ensure that the Trust will only receive income from the Health Commission in return for care delivered to patients in line with service contracts. This income will be passed on to Directorates and thence to Associate Directorates to fund the cost of delivery of care. It is unlikely that there will be any top slicing of funds to cover the costs of service departments such as Pharmacy or Personnel. It is believed by the managers concerned that these services will not survive in their current form or, be squeezed by increasing workloads or reducing resources available. The status quo is not seen as an option.

Guidance to answers to the questions set at the end of the case

Question 1

The activities of the two departments to date

Use of the models should enable students to identify the key issues that are affecting the Trust as a whole and then the pharmacy and personnel departments.

The pharmacy sees itself as being squeezed by financial and workload pressures and at the same time it is not delivering the management agenda which is controlling expenditure on medicines. Their motivation is to get close to customers with cash to spend, to influence the management agenda and, at the same time, find opportunities to streamline and develop services to meet other customer needs

The Personnel approach is more political. Although the Trust spends 70% of its revenue on staff the Personnel department see their strategic influence being eroded by the emergence of clinical directorates. They see themselves as being of use to directors in promoting manpower planning skill mix reviews etc. These differences in motivation provide the key to **Question 1**.

The strengths of the pharmacy approach is that they are seen to be customer focused but the process of interviewing customers is extremely time consuming. The personnel approach is more promotional and has communicated a message quickly, but may have communicated the wrong message to a cynical audience of managers. Promoting an *expanding role* message at a time of financial difficulty has been interpreted as empire building. This cynicism may not have been shared by the Trust Board who are themselves more 'mission focused'.

Question 2

Centralised or clinical directorate approach

This question is about how far the devolution process should go, and is it the same for different departments. There would appear to be benefits to getting closer to customers and being driven by their agenda:

- Front line staff who identify with the customer are likely to be seen by the customer to be achieving their objectives rather than those of their professional managers.

- Developments are more likely to be funded if they are identified by the customer and seen to be likely to achieve their results.

Disadvantages from the pharmacy and personnel managers point of view must be potential loss of control and reduction in flexibility in deploying staff, 'What do I do when staff in the pharmacy or personnel office are short and a member of staff is contracted to supply services to Department X?'

Students should identify these benefits and potential problems, weigh them up and suggest ways forward for each department. Is it possible to operate a 100 person organisation as a series of semi autonomous working teams and keep control?

111

Questions 3 and 4

The services from the customers point of view

These questions will require the student to get into the customer's mind and identify their requirements of each service.   A brainstorming technique is appropriate here, flagging up issues which are likely to be important to a busy doctor with limited time for a management role. Once the customer's requirements have been identified some proposals can be put forward as to how the service should be organised. The feedback from the doctors about pharmacy services is, 'We know who we like and we like who we know.' The indicators are towards devolution. This is intended to encourage a similar thought process for individuals in the group for their own working environment as well as in the case study.

Question 5

Selection and recruitment criteria for the future

Students should look at the new skill mix required by each department and how this can be achieved through recruitment and training.   This question centres around the attitudes, knowledge and skills required of individuals working in a devolved environment. Professional knowledge will have to be of the highest order because it will be "taken as read" by the clinical director. The directorate pharmacist or personnel officer will need to be streetwise, able to stand alone and make decisions with limited guidance from their parent department. In particular individuals will need to be outgoing, easy mixers with good presentation, influencing and negotiating skills. They will be expected to take manpower, budgetary and pharmaceutical data, validate it, interpret it and convert it into easily digestible information for the clinical directors. Recruitment should therefore concentrate on appointment of high calibre professional staff and training should concentrate on developing skills specific to the new style directorate posts.

KING CONCRETE — AN ANALYSIS OF THE BOUYGUES GROUP

Karen Meudell and Tony Callan

In order to answer the two questions posed, it is perhaps helpful to provide a brief overview of management 'life' in France [a more in-depth analysis is provided by Barsoux and Lawrence (1991) from which this synopsis is taken]

Leadership

The concept of the PDG (*Président-Directeur-Général*), often referred to as '*Le Patron*', is based on the *Führerprinzip* model imposed by the Vichy régime in 1940. Company law in France places in the hands of the individual what in most other countries is shared; Barsoux describes this as the 'Chairman of the Board and the Managing Director rolled into one' — '*Le patron règne en maître absolu*' ('The boss rules like a feudal overlord') who sees himself as responsible for the 'education' of his workforce.

This preparation for leadership is introduced and reinforced in the *Grandes Ecoles* (of which Francis Bouygues was a product) which confer confidence, provide a network of social contacts and allow for the occurrence of anticipatory socialisation where graduates assume, early on, the values, outlook and poise of the French 'ruling classes'.

Culture

There is a low level of social openness in France. A predilection for territory generally precludes open plan offices, there is little emphasis given to dialogue, teamwork and confrontation of opinions; a negative view is taken of conflict.

Equally there is considerable emphasis on secrecy, most large corporations shun publicity. This is probably for two reasons: the first to protect them from their competitors and the second because there is a general antipathy by the general public toward making money.

Corporate values are often an extension of family values with a desire for continuity and smooth succession — hence the concept of 'enlightened nepotism', where the heir to the throne is prepared from an early age.

The culture of lifelong employment is encouraged and devotion to work is actively promoted with many employees working anti-social hours (Barsoux suggests that this militates against women in France). Equally Job Descriptions are rare, as are precise organisation charts (described as organisational *flou* or vagueness). It would appear that this is favoured for two reasons: loyalty can be encouraged because positions are poorly defined and responsibilities are 'up for grabs', making internal promotion easier to manage.

Single product identity is encouraged rather than what is considered to be dilution by diversification.

Question 1

Evaluate the differences between the management styles of Martin and his father. What are the implications of these two styles for the culture and climate of the Bouygues Group?

F.B. can be seen as the archetypal French *Patron*, all seeing, all knowing, autocratic, paternalistic and encouraging feelings of élitism with his *Les Compagnons*. The resulting culture was a traditional power/web one with F.B. controlling the strands; this was typified by media speculation and the fall in share price when it was rumoured that he had died.

On the other hand, Martin's management style was much more collegiate in approach, his manner milder. He appears to have risen to his position through a combination, partly of inheritance (although we are told that he probably was not Francis' first choice for successor) and competence. He decided on the successful policy of diversification (an unusual one for French companies) and took the Company to even greater success. Whilst it can be argued that Martin's manner and policies would be more appropriate to a task culture, there is evidence that Martin is very much his father's son — his comment about being perceived as a "hunter" together with some of his seemingly impossible ideas are just two examples. The difference lies in Martin's ability to recognise that his management style has to be appropriate for the changing profile of the Group.

Mullins describes organisational climate as based on the perception of organisational members and characterised by the nature of people/organisational relationships — for example, structure, styles of leadership etc. A 'healthy' culture is based, in part, on: integration of personal and work goals, creating a sense of loyalty and identity; appropriate leadership; mutual trust; job design; equity in rewards, treatment and policies; opportunities for development and career progression and finally open discussion of conflict.

What is interesting in this particular case is that Bouygues, during Francis' time, appears to conform to the general model of French organisations, whilst running counter to everything Mullins suggests — indeed, the employee attitude survey cited in the case indicated that the organisation was promoting everything which Mullins decries. Students should be encouraged to explore this difference and suggest reasons why this should be so (see Further reading, below).

The implications of managing/working in a power culture are well documented [see, for example, Handy (1993)] and students should be encouraged to refer to this research and relate it to the Bouygues Group. Martin's very different approach is clearly indicated in the text of the case and students should be prompted to consider what would now be an appropriate culture for the new leadership. The obvious answer is a task culture, particularly in terms of managing the diversified organisation. However, once again it will be necessary to consider this overlaid on the traditional view of French management.

Question 2

One analyst suggests that Martin's policy makes Bouygues look more like a holding company than a construction firm. How appropriate is a power culture, typified by F.B.,

to the type of holding company that Martin appears to be developing? What difficulties might be anticipated and how might they be overcome?

Clearly a power culture would be totally inappropriate for the 'new' Bouygues if for no other reason than size. Handy suggests that the only way to prevent the web breaking is to spawn smaller webs linked to the main one. Whilst this is a possibility, it must be considered in the light of the other features of a power culture. Undoubtedly the culture needs to change, possibly to a task or, in some areas such as R&D, perhaps a matrix.

There are two further issues which need to be addressed:
(a)   managing the changes in both corporate leadership and strategy;
(b)   managing the diversified acquisitions to ensure that the organisation continues to develop in terms of its effectiveness.

(a)   These changes are appearing both from inside and outside. Change needs to be planned and have as its objectives the modification of members' behavioural patterns and the improved ability of the organisation to cope with its environment.

Success is more likely to be achieved if a participative management style is adopted. Therefore consideration should be given to the following:

- the creation of an environment of trust and shared commitment;
- active participation by everyone in the organisation;
- team management and a co-operative spirit.

This in itself would indicate that a change of culture is needed; the traditional power culture promoted by Francis needs to change, although some of the existing elements can be retained and encouraged — for example the Quality Circles programme, employee shareholding and the encouragement of training.

Attitude surveys should be utilised as a method of monitoring the changes.

(b)   The management of acquisition must take into account the two aspects of culture — organisational and national. Not only are organisations in different industries being acquired (for example, the Banco Centrale) but also in a variety of countries, each with its own national culture.

Areas which will need to be addressed will include:

- Integration of policies and procedures, although not necessarily to the point where they become common since this may result in a loss of flexibility.
- Socialisation of 'new' employees to the Group. This could be handled by, for example, cross-secondment of staff for a set period of time. This would also serve as a developmental process for the employees involved. Additionally, since history is frequently cited as a major determinant of culture, a readable/credible company history could be produced for these 'new' employees.
- An emphasis on communication, both informal and formal. Employees should be listened

to and informed regularly of any decisions or changes which are happening. Managers must be encouraged to 'walk the job' in order to obtain feedback and allay fears.
- Utilisation of existing staff rather than external recruitment. This will ensure that redundancies, either real or perceived, are minimised.

Further reading:

Hofstede, G. and Bond, M. H. (Spring). 'The Confucius connection: from cultural roots to economic growth', *Organizational Dynamics*, 16 pp. 5— 21.

Case 26

EXPERIENTIAL LEARNING AND THE LEARNING ORGANISATION

Brian McCormack and Linda McCormack

How the case can be used

The case presents a vehicle for exploring a range of issues including experiential learning, training evaluation and the learning organisation. In particular the tutor may wish to focus on:

- experiential learning activities integrated with business objectives;
- evaluation of learning activity;
- the parameters and frameworks they would use to decide to what extent the Collections Department of Club 24 had become a Learning Organisation.

Guidance for answers

Question 1

Stairway Framework

<u>Stage 1 Developing Commitment</u>

(a) Team building programmes for supervisors and managers to build a compelling vision of the future.

(b) Brainstorming workshops with all departmental teams to build commitment and identify core learning needs.

<u>Stage 2 Designing the Learning Intervention</u>

(a) Establishing key business objectives.
(b) Identifying current performance indicators.
(c) Identifying core learning modules.
(d) Learning methods and documentation.
(e) Developing group advisors.
(f) Venues and creation of a learning climate.

<u>Stage 3 Implementing 'Stairway'</u>

(a) Internal Marketing.
(b) Action planning as an integral feature of the project.

<u>Stage 4 Evaluating the Programme</u>

<u>Experiential Learning</u>

The experiential learning cycle is as shown in Figure 26.1.

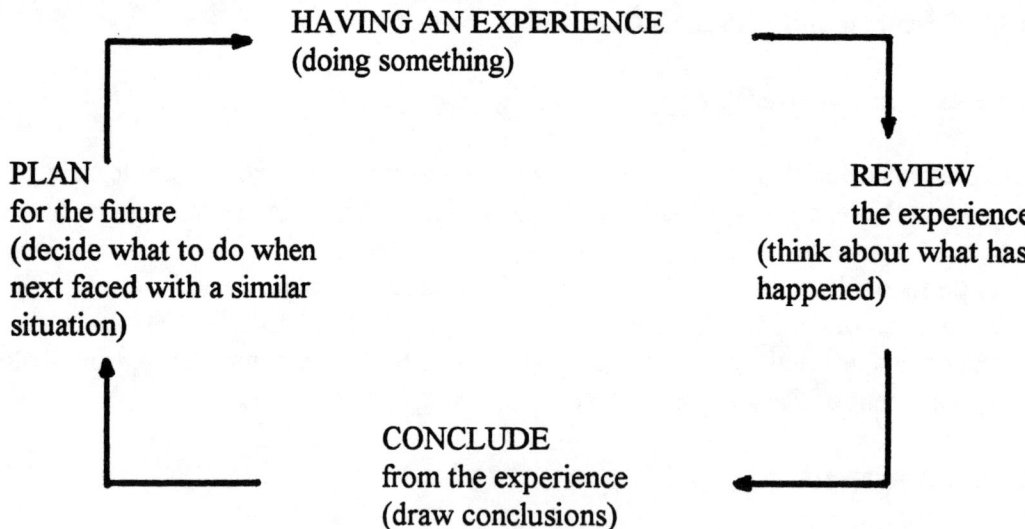

HAVING AN EXPERIENCE
(doing something)

PLAN
for the future
(decide what to do when
next faced with a similar
situation)

REVIEW
the experience
(think about what has
happened)

CONCLUDE
from the experience
(draw conclusions)

Fig 26.1

This cycle was built into on the job experience and off the job practice and exercises, e.g. role playing. On the job coaching as well as self evaluation enabled staff to learn from doing.

Question 2

(a)   Employee Evaluation.
        Special emphasis on coaching to embed learning.
(b)   Evaluation of Business Outcomes.
        Soft/hard measured eg. no. of collections, and short/long term considered.
(c)   Evaluation of Indirect Business Outcomes.
        Recognition of complex causal chains.
(d)   Group Advisors at Supervisory Level.
        Promote development as a continuous process by identifying reinforcing mechanisms.

Question 3

At the Continuation/Independency Stage, for example, the report can be used to highlight the organisational concerns and typical measures of achievement, e.g. BS5750, TQM and Investors in People.

What happened?

These quotations, from Ian Kendall can be related to Section 2, Stage 4 of Stairway, i.e. evaluating the programme.

'The chief reason for this [survival] has been the performance of the collections team

.... in terms of both the actual quantity of the money and the time in which they managed to achieve it. We'd like to say we're a long way there [towards becoming a learning organisation] .... we've got a long way to go.'

Other interviews indicated that not only single loop but also double loop learning was beginning to take root, i.e. the job holders were beginning to change the nature of their work and to improve the processes by which they were learning.

Some related theoretical considerations

This section locates the concept of the learning organisation in relevant theory and can be used as a framework for discussing the answers to the questions posed at the end of the case. A significant step forward was made in motivational theory when the model moved on from:

Dissatisfaction   --------------------->   Satisfaction

to:

      Hygiene factors
Dissatisfaction   --------------------->   No dissatisfaction

      Motivational factors
No Dissatisfaction   --------------------->   Satisfaction

In learning terms this can be translated to learning moving on from:

Poor Learning Culture --------------------->   Good Learning Culture

to:

     Remove Blocks -
     Unlearning
Poor Learning Culture --------------------->   Neutral Learning Culture

     Build Learning
Neutral Learning   --------------------->   Sustained Positive Culture
Culture

The poor learning climate is characterised by:
- lack of trust;
- lack of openness/communication;
- lack of shared beliefs/arms;
- lack of good systems.

Individuals

What has to be unlearned before learning can begin is different for different individuals in the organisation. For senior people relevant quotes are:

'Not enough resources', We are already doing it', 'new names for old techniques', 'what's it got to do with business/operations?', 'it is management's job to plan, organise, direct and control', and 'tell me exactly what it is you think we should do'.

For junior people relevant quotes are of the type:

'I do what I am told', 'I do my job - I wasn't recruited to do that', 'nobody wants m y ideas', 'I am not paid enough to worry', 'why should I let other people pick my brains, tell me what to do', 'I'll keep my head down and stay out of trouble', 'they're all looking out for their own status' and 'what's in it for me?'

Groups

In order to improve communications and trust, team building is often used; the idea often being to go from A to B in the diagram shown in Figure 26.2.

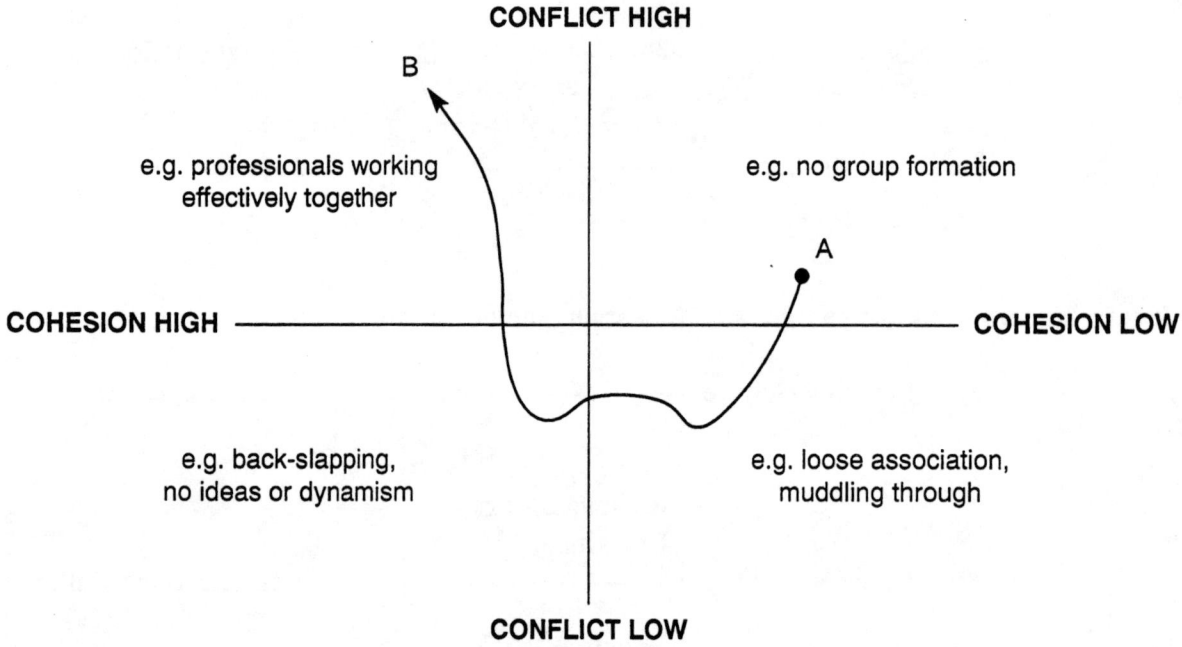

Fig. 26.2

Organisational

At the organisational level it is arguable that traditional functional lines of authority and structure, e.g. production, marketing, finance and personnel can inhibit learning. This block to the free-flow of ideas across, as well as up and down the organisation, can prevent the organisation evolving sufficiently in response to change. This lack of adaptation or learning can leave the organisation vulnerable.

Viewed as a whole other ways of allocating authority and responsibility became apparent, e.g. material resources, non-material resources (people and information), customers and the external environment, strategy and tactics, processes/procedures (e.g. BS 5750, TQM) and the internal customer, operations and last but not least — learning. These other views can be brought about by permanent structural changes or by temporary project teams and kept in existence until the change is felt to be permanent.

Change agent skills

Catalysts are usually required to trigger change. The following are quite common: internal champion, external pressure and internal crisis. Effective change agents usually have an excellent knowledge of organisational development techniques, experience of when to use what and good process skills (4) in order to create the right climate for high performance.

Summary

At one extreme the Learning Organisation concept can be seen as a new marketing fad; at the other extreme it can be viewed as a meta-theory under which a good deal of organisational development practice can be placed; as the latter could throw a good deal of light onto the relationship between current activities, e.g. the search for quality and investment in the workforce. The Learning Organisation idea can also be viewed as a natural development of organisational theory. Manufacture has progressed from being in the hands of the individual in cottage industries, through factories organised like machines to organisations using socio-technical systems theory, cybernetics, information and biology not only in manufacture but also as a metaphor for ways of organising.

If the firm can be considered as a brain, soft/hard systems theorists have been adapting brain models to organisational development for some time, then learning and its effective transmission to every part, i.e. total development is the key to the successful organisation.

Further reading

Garratt, R. (1990). *Creating a Learning Organisation: a guide to leadership*, Director Books.

Senge, P. M. (1990). *The Fifth Discipline: the art and practice (1990) of the Learning Organisation* Century Business.

Haslam, G. (1992). *The Learning Organisation: Holy Grail or Wholly Irrelevant?*, Durham University Business School, MBA Thesis.

Case 27

INVESTING IN PEOPLE: HUMAN RESOURCE DEVELOPMENT AND ORGANIZATIONAL CHANGE

David Goss

How the case can be used

The case portrays attempts by two companies to introduce organizational change through an HRD initiative. The vehicle in both was the IIP scheme which provides a common base against which the success of the change programmes can be assessed. Although seeking to meet a common set of standards laid down by the IIP initiative, the problems and issues faced by the companies were very different. Thus the case provides an opportunity to examine the benefits and costs associated with such strategies.

Answers to activity brief questions

Question 1

There are a number of factors which may contribute to these differing experiences of the IIP initiative. The ones that seemed to be most significant in the actual cases were the role of senior managers (see **Question 2.**), the size of the organizations and, especially, the role played by personnel specialists. The effect of size was mostly in terms of the additional administrative loading that was created by the need to prepare detailed portfolios of evidence covering all employees. More significant seemed to be the role of personnel specialists. Thus, in the first case, IIP was seen as an unnecessary intrusion into an already existing system and as a potential threat to the position on that system. In this respect the changes necessary to comply with the IIP standard were seen in terms of 'adjustments' to existing systems rather than new developments. In the second case, however, it filled a developing void and, in this respect, the changes IIP initiated were perceived to be both fundamental and beneficial. Thus, it can be suggested that the success of IIP is heavily conditioned by an organization's internal politics, especially those associated with existing personnel policy.

Here it may be useful to consider theories of conflict and power [Mullins (1993), Kolb and Bartunek (1992), Sims et al (1993), Clegg (1989)].

Question 2

What do the cases reveal about the role of top managers in change processes?

The other factor which appeared to shape the acceptance of IIP was the role and attitude of the top managers. In the first case, this was one of limited personal commitment: IIP was 'imposed' for largely instrumental reasons and no real steps were taken to gain the support of lower level managers other than to ensure their compliance. Thus, while 'lip-service' was paid to the initiative, few people felt that it was genuinely a key concern, hence the widespread cynicism. The approach in the second case was to drive IIP strongly from the very top and to make it absolutely clear that the initiative was crucially important and that, for managers especially, it would form a component of their performance appraisal. This drive appeared to be crucial in overcoming the 'political' objections and scepticism towards IIP in its early stages.

Clearly this relates most directly to debates about 'transformational leadership', although an understanding of the nature of employee commitment and effects of organizational culture may also be used to analyse this issue [Goss (1994), Pheysey (1993), Coopey and Hartley (1991), Morgan (1986)].

Question 3

Does IIP point the way towards a system of human resource management without personnel specialists?

Here the emphasis should be on the implications of the 'transparency' of employment relations and objectives that is implicit in the IIP rationale. For example, to what extent does the commitment to the explicit formulation of employee roles and responsibilities in terms of core business objectives demand that responsibility for human resource management must rest with line managers? Similarly, does the emphasis on systematic monitoring and evaluation of human resource performance point towards a regime where personnel specialists are irrelevant as a result of the simultaneous 'empowerment' of line managers and their subordinates: the latter as a result of a heightened awareness of human resource issues and their management; the latter as a consequence of increased understanding of their role and contribution to organizational objectives?

This has relevance to current debates about Human Resource Management (HRM) [Goss (1994), Legge (1989), Blyton (1992), Towers (1992), Boxall (1992), Marlow and Patton (1993)].

Question 4

Both cases are based on the views of senior managers. What cautions should this suggest when it comes to interpreting their views?

The obvious problem with accepting the views of senior managers is that they may have a vested interest in presenting strategy/policy decisions in a light which either removes them from blame or places them in a favourable light. This is a n especial problem with the second case where it could legitimately be claimed that it would be necessary to seek the views of the employees affected before accepting the stated benefits of IIP.

Further reading

Mullins, L. J. (1993). *Management and Organisational Behaviour*, London: Pitman, Chapter 20.

Kolb, D. and Bartunek, J. (Eds) (1992). *Hidden Conflict in Organizations*, London: Sage.

Sims, J., Fineman, S. and Gabriel, J. (1993). *Organizing and Organizations*, London: Sage.

Clegg, S. (1989). *Frameworks of Power*, London: Sage.

Goss, D. (1994). *Principles of Human Resource Management*, London: Routledge.

Pheysey, D. (1993). *Organizational Cultures*, London: Routledge.

Coopey, J. and Hartley, J. (1991). 'Reconsidering the case for organizational commitment', *Human Resource Management Journal*, 1, 13, pp. 18—32.

Morgan, G. (1986). *Images of Organization*, London: Sage.

Legge, K. (1989). 'Human resource management: a critical analysis', in Storey, J. (Ed). *New Developments in Human Resource Management*, London: Routledge.

Blyton, P. (Ed) (1992). *Reassessing Human Resource Management*, London: Sage.

Towers, B. (Ed) (1992). *Handbook of Human Resource management*, Oxford: Blackwell.

Boxall, P. (1992). 'Strategic human resource management: beginnings of a new theoretical sophistication', *Human Resource management Journal*, 2, 3, pp. 60—79.

Marlow, S. and Patton, D. (1993). 'Managing the employment relation in small firms: possibilities for HRM', *International Small Business Journal*, 11; 4, pp. 57—64.